TYRONE FOLK QUEST

Michael J Murphy

Blackstaff Press Belfast

© Michael J Murphy 1973

All rights reserved. No part of this publication may be reproduced, stored in a retrieval system or transmitted, in any form or by any means, electronic, mechanical, photocopying, recording or otherwise, without the prior permission of Blackstaff Press Ltd.

Published by Blackstaff Press Limited, 16 Donegall Square South, Belfast BT1 5JF with the assistance of the Arts Council of Northern Ireland.

First impression 1973
Second impression 1974

British Library Cataloguing in Publication Data

Murphy, Michael J. (Michael Joseph), *1913 –*
  Tyrone folk quest
  1. Folk-lore – Ireland – Tyrone County
  I. Title
  398'.092'4   GR148.T/

ISBN 0-85640-038-6

First published in 1973
by The Blackstaff Press
with the assistance of The Arts Council of Northern Ireland

Reissued with corrections in 1983
by The Blackstaff Press
3 Galway Park, Dundonald, Belfast BT16 0AN

© Michael J. Murphy, 1973
All rights reserved

Printed in Northern Ireland by The Universities Press Limited

The publishers would like to thank An Chomhairle Ealaíon
for permission to reproduce the cover painting,
'The Black Lake' by Gerard Dillon.

CONTENTS

		Page
1	To Go or Not To Go	7
2	Folklore Flitting	9
3	'Only a Stranger Here'	12
4	'The Bungalow'	14
5	The Man Who Followed the Fairies	16
6	Glenhull	18
7	Meeting the People	19
8	The Quest Begins	23
9	An Able Storyteller	25
10	Reds in Glenhull	27
11	Padraig McCullagh of Curraghinalt: Craftsman	30
12	Collecting in Earnest	35
13	The Delicate Tread of Sex	38
14	Advent of Spring	40
15	The Stations	42
16	Glenlark	46
17	Man With a Sense of Humour	49
18	'Ploughin' The Headrig Anymore'	51
19	Interlude in Lore-Hunting	54
20	The Last Druid in Ireland	55
21	Cromwell and The Irish Dead	57
22	People From Home	61
23	Heinrich Wagner and The Gaelic Speakers	63
24	The Break	68
25	A Tale of Two Typewriters	70
26	A Man of Stones	72
27	A Killing on The Road to Rome	74
28	Following Fairies Further A-Field	75
29	Tinker Trouble	79
30	Turn of The Year and The Naghan tuighe Mhuire	80
31	Fowl Play	83
32	The White Bird of The Lowlands	85
33	The Broad Road Again	87
34	The First Farewell	90
35	The Folk Mind Closes	92
36	End of a Quest	94
37	The Return	94

DEDICATION

*To my wife and our Tyrone
neighbours and storytellers alive and dead:
without all their help this work
and the folklore volumes they helped me amass
would have gone unrecorded . . . for ever.*

NOTE

Each collector for the former Irish Folklore Commission, now incorporated into the newly created Department of Irish Folklore at University College, Dublin, was required to keep a daily Journal as well as writing or transcribing normal collections of folklore. The idea behind the project of compiling such social documentaries on bearers of tradition was introduced and encouraged by Professor Seamus Delargy, Director of the Folklore Commission, and is endorsed by his successor in the Department of Irish Folklore, Professor Bo Almqvist, Fil. dr. (Uppsala).

This present work is based on two such hand-written Journals covering the period 1949 to 1952 in Glenhull and the surrounding areas in Co. Tyrone. Stray items of folklore appearing are incidental: the work proposes instead to deal mainly with the storytellers who told folklore to the writer and his wife, their own reactions to these people; and the associated events involved in integrating, for a special purpose, in the community of a remote mountainous district in Ulster.

It is hoped also that the work may afford some insight into the background and aspirations, the problems and intellectual excitements of at least one contemporary folklorist in the field.

Michael J. Murphy,
Dromintee,
South Armagh. *March,* 1973

1 To Go or Not To Go

'... These collections of yours are probably the most valuable documentation of oral tradition which has ever been made in the English-speaking districts of Ulster...'

Or, unfortunately, ever likely to be made: I was in at the Death.

The above report, from the Irish Folklore Commission in the 1950's, could never have been written had my wife and I not decided to go to live in Glenhull in Co. Tyrone: written that is, with the assurance it carries. I could have gone alone as I had to the Mournes in 1945, walking with an ash-plant: useful, surely, but without yielding the satisfying results of depth inquiry which derives from true integration into a community.

In Dublin I had agreed to go to the Sperrins in Tyrone for two years: 'a cultural intelligence officer' as Seamus Delargy had put it: with my knowledge of the nuances of the intimate realities of rural life, people I had yet to meet were to open heart and folk mind to me. Telling their own history for the first time they would, in fact, have to make a confession of their spiritual and social soul intertwined by pre-Christian beliefs and cultures. Having been reared around Slieve Gullion's foot in South Armagh, and my wife in Faughart in North Louth, we knew what the rural mind and its secret recesses could be like. But we would have to approach this quest together.

That was December in 1949. We had arranged to go on the 13th. Early morning of that date was miserable with rain around Slieve Gullion, which rose beyond a few rough fields across from our back window. Alice and I sat before the open fire in silence listening to the downpour slush the window and pelt the roof. The time was around 6.00 am. In half an hour a lorry on its way to Cookstown in Tyrone was willing to oblige me by making a detour to Glenhull in the southern foothills of the Sperrins and would take me and the furniture along... If we had decided to go.

I couldn't decide.

We didn't own the house we lived in and would leave it without much regret especially to the rats which peered down at night from holes in the felt ceiling. But I was used to flitting: my wife was not, and she had been seriously ill all summer. Our youngest boy was just two months, the eldest three years old. I would bring them to a remote Tyrone glen in the Sperrins to a house they had never seen; I had merely seen the outside on my sole visit to the place after a bicycle ride of twenty miles from Omagh. It had been closed for two years; unlike the other houses on the hillside it stood alone alongside the road. It would be cold, damp and unaired: shutters (and a defective key) prevented my seeing the state of it inside. Since 1922 when I had been 'brought home' from Liverpool, where I was born, to Slieve Gullion in South Armagh, I had had a varied knowledge of unaired country houses and had no illusions left. Furthermore, I knew no one in Glenhull in Tyrone and no one knew me.

Alice said that she would like to be settled in the place for Christmas.

I knew why I hesitated: integration in a new community would mean dis-integrating myself from the mystic moods of the Slieve Gullion valley.

I was also the most parochial man alive: the rims of our circle of hills confined my content. At the outskirts of my own parish I felt a stranger...

She insisted that we go. She believed I had become too immersed in the moods and mystery of life and land in South Armagh.

At half-past six it still poured into pitch dark. Nothing could be seen from either back or front window except the rain and the reflections of the oil-lamp and the firelight from the open grate under the crane and crooks which held kettle or pot over the blaze.

I began to wonder if the lorry-man would go on such a morning. But they had assured Alice the night before that they would: I was to be at the end of our lane to give our decision. They were going to haul lime from outside Cookstown in a high, stubby, iron-bodied truck known then as a 'Burma Ford' reputedly designed for fast, tough service during World War II. This run would be their last until spring. No other vehicle from our Slieve Gullion country touched on Tyrone, while official hauliers stipulated that before undertaking a removal I must give assurance (which I could not) of accessible approach to both houses. I hadn't been to Glenhull when first I inquired, nor could any ordinary lorry reach our house in South Armagh along the crooked, narrow lane. (Anyhow, the official reply to one inquiry about transport didn't reach me until I was settled in Glenhull weeks later.)

The dead-line came and Alice still insisted that we go. From the window I watched for the sign of headlights inflaming the rain-soaked heavens over the bog-road beyond our front window. My father lived nearby and I had promised to let him know early if we had decided to flit. A niece of mine, Brigid O'Hare, had volunteered to help Alice with the three children down to Glenhull. I would ride ahead in the lorry and have the house open and at least a fire going when they arrived.

The children now had to be roused; a quick breakfast made; articles and gear packed. I had known some hurried flittings, but none so hectic as this one. Behind it all I concealed a terrible concern and apprehension.

From the open doorway rain fell on to the threshold like quivering steel rods. No sign of light shone anywhere in the blackness, except an occasional glare of reflection from the townlights of Dundalk six miles beyond the hilltop of The Dhaaicklemore, the glare coming and going as the density of the rain-clouds teased and bulked up again.

2 Folklore Flitting

I helped to pack and took some breakfast on my feet. The children were bewildered, still half-asleep; the eldest, Patrick, suspiciously and in subdued alarm, eyed the disarray. I understood; and remembered being hauled 'home' from Liverpool in 1922 – tubbed and scrubbed on a wrong night in mid-week, puzzled and bewildered even next morning when my mother held out new clothes and said:

'Come on, *avick*. Out of my clothes and into your own. We're going home.'

But I had been nine years old; Patrick was three. I had also known folklore without knowing what it was; without ever having heard the name uttered. No one, in fact, would have understood if the word had cropped up. Yet I had been born into the cult across the Irish Sea in Liverpool. My parents and relatives, all Irish emigrants, used to gather in for a fireside ceili: I had heard that word. No one deliberately urged that I should listen. But from a seat on our fender around the range of our hearth in Eden Street in Liverpool I heard other idioms and had them explained later by my mother. I used to hear my father, a seaman, talk as they talked. His own grandfather, William Jordan, had been a South Armagh Gaelic scribe. Without knowing it I heard my father tell the first folk story I was to hear, as well as general tradition about the birth place at Slieve Gullion in their native South Armagh.

Home to South Armagh in 1922, storytelling and traditional belief and practice were still living cults: my father was back at sea, but my mother began to observe customs and passing beliefs we had never heard about in Liverpool. I was in the habitat of events and customs I had heard them talk about: where to walk at night on lonely roads to avoid ghosts – walk where the horse or ass walked, not in wheel tracks; how to behave at a wake; what to say in a house where churning was going on; how hatching hens should be 'set' on a clutch, and when, and why ashes and Holy Water and a piece of iron had to be used on the nest. And so on.

Yet no one ever mentioned the word 'folklore'. I don't even remember having heard it in school. When I left school and went to work for local farmers there was the attraction of new lore to be heard from men and women who were my work companions. I began to note it all down, still unaware of the term 'folklore'.

The strange mood of Slieve Gullion and the land it influenced began to intrigue me. I tried to interpret this amid work in the bog and mountain fields in terms of tradition heard or in evocative prose-poems, especially at harvest which particularly moved and excited me. I was thrilled when one such piece brought me a letter from Maud Gonne MacBride who wrote:

'... I have read your article "The Eve of Harvest" and I think we share many thoughts, though you are young and I am so old and tired. I understand so well how some little thing like your head of shot grain can evoke a dream more vivid than what we sometimes call reality, and take one into the World where Time is not and you have the rare power of describing it ...'

I could have related that properly to the thing Folk, but I still had not heard the word 'folklore'. Only when my book, *At Slieve Gullion's Foot*, was published in 1942 did I hear of the Irish Folklore Commission when Professor Seamus Delargy asked me to collect on a part-time basis around my own parish.

It was only then that I began to believe I understood a profound truth. More by instinct than analysis I was convinced that the thing folk enshrined the seminal strains fundamental to the essential philosophy of the people: that it retained and motivated a mental blue-print of much contemporary impulse and idea. This was a revelation which excited me; but the full import of what it meant and connoted really impressed me when I began to work among the people of Glenhull in Tyrone. Later research elsewhere confirmed the instinctive impressions.

We did not know anyone in Glenhull in Tyrone. I had gone alone to Omagh to sound out the possibilities of respective areas. I knew that Mick Murphy (no relation) the publican in Mill Street in Newry had been in Tyrone. He gave me a few names of people I should see and who in turn, he hoped, would help. In Omagh I saw the advertisement of a house to let in Glenhull. Where was Glenhull? I borrowed a bike and set off to find it.

I couldn't get into the house as the key I had been given wouldn't fit. I reported back to Alice. She suggested that I take the house nevertheless. We would be two years there. Neither of us dreamt that we were to rediscover a Folk Kingdom clutching to its last threads of life: or that the proposed two years would extend to more than twenty and would cover folklore collecting in areas of Old Ulster from Rathlin to The Boyne, from Strangford Lough to Glangevlin in Cavan and to Leitrim and Sooey in County Sligo.

In December of 1949 that was in the future, however. The people of Glenhull in Tyrone were to widen my own experience in preparation for that future.

When I saw the lights of the lorry probe the teeming swabs of cloud over the bog I called from the doorway that I was going to waken my father. The old lane, as my father would have said in seafaring argot 'was a-wash'. How many times had I carried sacks of coal up it from the road over the rough stones and ruts? No motor lorry would attempt it. Half-way down I met my father coming up; he had been watching as well.

He had retired from the sea – forcibly on 'the dole' and then on his old age pension. When my younger sister and my mother died within three days of each other the shock had hit him hard. He had never forgotten country skills and manners and tales although he had sailed the seas of the world. As a youth he had been a pedlar along with his own father in the Highlands of Scotland and had traditions from that Celtic belt as well. Like myself he had a social conscience and had been on strikes in Dublin with Big Jim Larkin, whose people were from beside us in Killeavy in South Armagh. Quiet, good company, shy. (Another South Armagh seaman first told me how my father, none too sober, on a doped Mediterranean wine, had 'knocked a jaunty-arm' (gendarme) into a navigable river and then jumped in after him, forgetting that he couldn't swim a stroke.)

When I got to the end of the lane the lorry was waiting on the road outside the gate ('The gate' was, in fact, an iron hurdle looted during the Black and Tan War from Lord Claremont's demesne just across the border in Ravensdale in Co. Louth following the burning of the Big House by local Republicans.)

Yes, we had decided to flit: they had come prepared with a good cover. But could they, I asked, get along the narrow lane between its stone ditches? They had inspected it the previous night: the metal sides of the truck could squeeze and take a scrape if they had to. I was told to go back and prepare and leave the rest to them.

I finished my breakfast on my feet. The children were whimpering, my father soothing them as he helped Alice to pack. A kind of terror kept Patrick's dark eyes wide. When the lorry with a metallic rumble and roar of powerful motor squelched close to the threshold he yelled and bolted to roost on the rungs which stretched under the big table. (On these rungs in the old days a corpse used to be laid out.)

The flitting began. Beds were hurriedly dismantled and hauled out to the lorry. Ticking and bed-clothes were shouldered in a crush through the doorway in a quick dash to toss the burden under the cover on the lorry. Delph was being packed in a large crock which normally held the well-water. Much as I should have been accustomed to a flitting I could never reconcile myself to the sense of stupefaction which fills the vacuum as pieces of furniture are removed. Patrick saw this; thought no doubt strange men were pulling the place down, and worse than all we were helping.

Someone finally asked about my books. I didn't have many but made a rapid choice, filled two old suitcases, and left the remainder to be collected later. I have never seen them since. My typewriter went out in its wooden case which I had fashioned from two war-time ammunition boxes: I used to haul it around in a cardboard carton until one day in a crowded bus going to the Mournes a large jovial woman wanted to know why she wasn't allowed to sit on it. And sat.

Decision had to be made as to what to take and what to abandon, for already the lorry was as high as a newly built stack. The deluge continued. Iron three-legged pots and pot-ovens went in along with the griddle – even the Hanging Dresser, which was to intrigue Tyrone friends as yet unknown. The big table would have to remain. I almost forgot to fetch coal in sacks.

By the time Brigid O'Hare arrived, no doubt wondering what she had let herself in for, the lorry was ready to leave. Then there was a cry and someone handed me the pan, still hot.

My father said to me quietly:

'I can only wish yous the height of good luck. You're not missin' much in this oul' hole of a house in the hollow anyway.' He went on: 'I'll miss the children. The boys'll maybe miss me, I'd say. But,' he added quickly, 'I'll be down to see yous all in the Spring when the weather mends – if God spares me.'

We were ready to go. Rain still poured out of the blackness. Alice with Brigid O'Hare and the family would go by taxi and train and taxi again. I would see them in Glenhull. It was then like saying 'the moon'. Where was

Glenhull . . . ? Being committed I think I was really scared for a moment.

The lorry edged away lumbering, bumping, squelching along the lane and on to the road, facing north. My father and I shook hands. I was leaving him for the first time, instead of he leaving me as when I used to help him with his seabag as far as Dundalk. I climbed in, waved as he stood in the rain in the reflection of the headlights, and we were off.

And if no one knew me in Glenhull, or expected my arrival, only then did I realise that no one except my own family knew I was leaving Slieve Gullion. The old mountain was hidden behind the tattered cloaks of the rain clouds.

3 'Only a Stranger Here'

From Dromintee at Slieve Gullion in South Armagh to Glenhull in North Tyrone cannot be more than eighty miles; but when moving in Ireland to take up residence distance cannot be assessed in mere miles.

I had heard a man from Co Mayo say in South Armagh, when asked to give some opinion affecting social relationship, 'I'm only a stranger here.' Yet he had lived in our parish for about forty years. I had heard people say much the same sort of thing when they had moved from one end of the parish to another, and certainly if they had moved to another parish.

The same attitude is common throughout all Ireland and may be attributed to social causes traced to an arbitrary and instinctive interpretation of the old clan spirit and its diversified code of loyalites. These began with the family, extended to the townland, then the parish or district (especially if it has an old territorial title such as Muintire Linney which encompasses Glenhull in Tyrone) and so on to include the county and finally the province.

We sped through the village of Meigh and on to Newry. The blackness of the December night and morning was lifting, but the rain stayed. I was asked about Glenhull and the best way to get there across country but did not know. I knew that if we could reach the wee town of Carrickmore in Tyrone a road across the wide open Black Bog would lead us near the glen at Greencastle.

On my only visit to Glenhull I had come from Omagh on a bicycle loaned me by the son of the landlord, the late Dan McCrae. He hadn't been in his bar when I called to make inquiries about the house to let. Hearing my South Armagh accent people refuted my claim to have come from 'the North' and claimed my accent indicated Sligo. In Dan McCrae's they had taken another impression – to quote Dan later:

They had said I 'sounded like an Englishman' to which he had rejoined:

'Then that rules him out. No Englishman will ever live out there in Glenhull.'

We drove through Richill. Plantation country from which our forebears had been ousted into the hills in the south. To us at Slieve Gullion in South Armagh this was 'the North', the land which absorbed the hired servant boys and girls on 'The Hiring Ground' in Newry, work-twisted and tongue-twisted them for six months and a pittance of wages and then let them loose. My mother and father, at ten years of age, had worked in the same broad rich acres and the Mournes near Hilltown. My mother had pleaded with me never to work in the fields at home. 'The last coach bar the hearse' was the traditional phrase she used to decry it. When I went to work for farmers it was a case of wages needed, not experience. But above all I had had to promise 'never to go "Down the North" or stand on a Hiring Ground with my bundle in my oxter'.

I was on my way North after all.

The rain stopped as we drove through Armagh on to Dungannon, through Carrickmore where our flapping high load almost sent a horse and cart in fright over the bank into the bog – and on to Greencastle. Inquiring the way at one house I wondered why the woman stared at me over her half-door. I hadn't washed after the flitting from Dromintee; as well as being wet I was as black with coal and soot as the Earl of Hell's waistcoat or a coalheaver after a dirty shift.

We were behind schedule, having lost our way earlier outside Dungannon. We sped through Creggan. Far ahead in the rising cloud to the north were the hillsides rising out of the glens, with the mountains of Sawel and Dart rearing high in the background.

Almost at once the two men beside me in the cabin exclaimed as if in alarm:

'Look begod! Snow!'

Not only on Sawel and Dart, but in banks along the roadside. I almost felt as if I must accept some responsibility: no snow had appeared in South Armagh.

Through Greencastle, hamlet with a pub and shop, up and over a hill; and there far below lay Glenhull and the house we were going to – a dull grey blob. Snow lay around the fields.

(On their return to Dromintee the men, neighbours named Connolly, opined: 'We'll give him a month in thon place.' Meaning that I would flee out as I was now in a sense fleeing into it.)

Down the hill; past Morris's shop: past McCullagh's corn-grinding mill, its massive waterwheel turning; past McCrae's pub and the post-office and not another house until we reached 'The Bungalow,' as people referred to our new abode. Actually, it had been designed as a shop and store but never used for that purpose.

There was a small iron gate and a few concrete steps leading to a steep, overgrown track. Mounds of bleached grasses and weeds tripped us. The house was a cold grey, concreted, but with a sound-looking slate roof. The windows, though shuttered, looked large. The doorway, unusually tall for one in a country house, lacked paint. There was a winter-bare hawthorn hedge along the road. A mountain stream ran close to one gable along a ditch.

I was as eager to get in and settled and get a fire lighted as the men were to get away. I fished out a second key given to me by my landlord in Omagh.

It wouldn't fit either.

4 'The Bungalow'

The shutters were secured with six-inch nails driven home. But there was a back door fastened with a 'hanging lock' and chain attached by steeples to the door-check. A surprisingly simple bit of 'breaking and entering' – with the tang of a file I found lying by – withdrew the steeples. Rain had started again. I shouldered my way in.

A long concrete passage as smooth as glass and four feet wide led from door to door. I opened the front door. Bedding and bed-clothes were rushed in as they had been rushed out in Dromintee. Articles of furniture were stacked everywhere and anywhere. Finally, to take a breath, one of the lorry-men sat on a piece of sacking on some article: it was shielding a wedding-present mirror which cracked in two. No one bothered to comment or mumble embarrassed excuse or apology.

We looked around the place. Though the shutters were still in place slits let in a fair light. The ravages of damp were everywhere. No one spoke. Two flakings as big as table-tops bulged on either side of the chimney. Others here and there had dropped off walls originally white-washed.

The fireside was simple and familiar: a large smithy-made grate set in two hobs, with swinging iron crane and crooks. Twigs, debris and sheeps' wool in the grate reminded me at once of a chimney blocked with heaven knows how many Jackdaws' nests.

The place consisted of a kitchen-cum-living room and two bedrooms. The kitchen was long and narrow. The windows unusually large (the place, as I've said, had been designed as a shop) one opposite each other, each consisting of two panes. Apart from an old table and an iron-rod fireguard in a corner in the darkness the place was bare, without cupboard or in-built press of any kind.

A raw-boarded partition separated the kitchen from the passageway between it and the rooms. Each had a sound, boarded floor, with a good window, but only the larger room had a fireplace. With renewed dismay I noticed once again the twigs from old nests like a down-thrust of wire bursting out of a casing. Damp had gouged plaster from the walls. When I fingered other suspected spots pulverised plaster trickled like meal spurting from a rip in a sack.

It was now time for the lorry-men to go. We exchanged laconic 'So longs', they wished me luck and drove off. I don't remember having felt so alone in my life.

I started on the kitchen fireplace first, pulling armfuls of thorny twigs out of the mouth of the chimney. It stayed blocked. Again and again I blindly mauled down twigs, horse dung balls and wool. Still no sign of light; it was high and narrow, not the familiar barrow-wide maw characteristic of the traditional country houses I had known. I thought of burning, but fire was dangerous unless one knew the height of possible exposed roof timbers in the chimney. Somewhere outside in the rain, falling lightly now, I plundered a light pole. In the end I could have cheered when the last of the twigs collapsed and daylight, grey and bleary, showed above me. At least I had a soot-free chimney now. I started a fire and tackled the room chimney.

It was impossible to see up this one and I worked like a miner in a confined shaft, tossing twigs and dry dung, rags, paper and sheeps' wool over my shoulder. The room floor began to fill up. My plundered pole was of no use. I found a length of paling wire and used it, and, when I believed – and hoped – the last of the obstruction had been removed, lighted a fire and went to get the shutters off.

When at last I got one shutter off the front window of the kitchen I saw more trouble: a heap of hard-packed animal dung in the corner, inside the fireguard. (Some previous tenant had kept a calf in that corner with the fireguard to contain the animal; a practice which had, admittedly, a traditional background, but hardly to the extent to which such a heap of manure could testify.) Using a slit sack as carrier I spaded out the plaster debris, the dirt and the dung and the fire was roaring when, at dusk, my family arrived from Omagh station in a taxi at the gate. Even the taxi man had had to inquire for Glenhull.

Alice was carrying Peter, the infant, in a tartan shawl. Brigid O'Hare was handling the other two, Patrick still in wide-eyed bewilderment and alarm, Michael exhausted in a half-doze, but smiling. Then Alice stopped and nodded at the house. I turned.

With the insidious (and sardonic) slither of a menacing summer mist through mountain-peak rocks, smoke crept from under every slate over the room, even from behind the frame and sashes of the window. My hopes were wrong; the chimney was still blocked. This meant that all of us would have to bed down in the kitchen for the night. (Actually we had to do so for a week.)

Yet Alice said she liked the place. I mentioned the falling plaster but she reminded me that we knew a traditional method of dealing with that. Brigid O'Hare said nothing; she had good grounds for believing that she had let herself in for a kind of weird penitential pilgrimage in the cause of Irish folk culture. But she did not complain.

First of all food was cooked amid the cluster of furniture. Clothes were aired. Confusion was righted when a sought article was found, to become confused again when something needed was found missing – abandoned in Dromintee. The children now were too exhausted to bother us. It was time to rest. I got up several times through the night to refuel the fire, but awakened no one. We slept the 'sleep of the dead' on that first night in Glenhull in Tyrone.

5   The Man Who Followed the Fairies

At this point something need be said about folklore itself and the folklore collector.

When I first began to collect outside my own district in South Armagh and went walking through the Mournes I knew I had become known as 'The Man Who Was Following the Fairies'. (Just as in Glenhull in Tyrone I was to be referred to normally as 'The Bungalow Man After Folklore' or even merely 'The Bungalow Man'. The rural mind has a neat aptitude for inventing traditional tags to use as vivid identifying labels for person and place, for event and crises, both past and present.)

But while Fairy-lore is an important section of the national folk heritage it also provides evidence to the anthropologist – and now no doubt for the psycho-analytic historian. Just the same the scamper of our flitting to Glenhull could seem wildly exaggerated even for such a scientific purpose and the collection of all folklore in general. The fact is that the popular mind even today – in town *and* countryside – persists in equating folklore exclusively with the fairy-story, with custom and mythical belief, with the ghost and the folk-tale.

That it has developed into a vast and intimate and intricate social survey finds little credence with the popular mind. The fault is partly because of the approach to the work by the folklore collector. The dedicated folklore collector should avoid popular publicity on any media like a man on the run: should work like a poteen-maker in his den. He has to win the confidence of people adroitly, and patiently be able to ask them to confess to a knowledge which, if breathed abroad, can bring down the wrath of friend and neighbour, of priest or parson – even policeman. He wants not only the *tales* people can remember and narrate but just as important the *details* of their lives and living as well, their very thoughts and attitudes to all kinds of human, social and religious concepts – and the same of their peoples' people as far back as the human memory can reach. He must nevertheless have that extraordinary patience and the ability of an actor: he must arrange for people to get to know him rather than he getting to know the people: must assure them by behaviour as well as by word of an absolute respect for secrecy. He must never show tiredness or boredom or irritation. An understanding of the urgency and importance of his work must retrieve and sustain a collapsing patience.

He must know how to tread delicately: he is intruding on the souls of a people. A Christian people have to be induced to confess to a knowledge and unspoken respect for essentially pagan beliefs and practices, even concepts sometimes in conflict with established religious authority: in conflict indeed with contemporary social norms and practices: often in confused conflict with evolving attitudes of their own. Sex beliefs and practices, for instance, aphrodisiacs, contraceptive and abortion information known and practised covertly comprise only one sub-section of the Hidden Mind of the real Hidden Ireland: the so-called Preserve of the Simple-Minded Peasant.

This so-called simple-minded peasant (if we ever really had a true peasantry) is in fact pure myth inasmuch as such a mind is at least the most complex mental machine one can encounter. It is admittedly taciturn and evasive. Some people interested in tradition, even people brought up in rural Ireland – particularly since the 1920s – do not believe or even suspect the existence of this social phenomenon. Similar communities throughout Europe have, of course, the same protective evasiveness. In our own environment some school-teachers and doctors, and clergymen especially, repudiate the claim that such a mental layer with its associate attitudes and knowledge ever existed.

There are reasons. To be brief, the folk mind still fears exposure or ridicule. It nurses its secrets. The same aspect or attitude in the folk mind which still attributes supernatural or extraordinary curative powers to the unfrocked or 'silenced' priest nevertheless excludes from its circle of secrets the future priest, school-master or doctor, or indeed anyone who would tend to rise out of its class. Even a writer from among the rural people can find exclusion insidiously shutting him out; as if he or she were one about to betray the collective hoard of the recesses of the mind of a folk community. All rural peoples are still that.

From the '20s especially pupils left their home place for secondary school or college or seminary much earlier than in previous decades; thus they were cut off from an adult understanding of the free and uninhibited talk in topics of fireside and field. There are other factors, but these would merely extend the generalisations which must be inevitable here: yet I have seen this reaction of the inner cores of the folk mind manoeuvre courteously time and again. I knew for instance an old Parish Priest who had once been rural enough to have had his Dues paid in oats. ('The Priest's Wite' they called this sieve-like article in South Armagh.) He was eager to hear folklore being told. But the ceili disappointed him sadly, as I knew it must. Only when he had become bored and had left were chairs drawn up and the real talk among the people, his parishioners, began.

Collectively the folk mind – even now in its final disarray – is still an astounding survival of ideas and racial memories retained in depth and detail and approach. The belief in the supernatural powers of the unfrocked priest has been mentioned for example: this represents perhaps a mental throw-back of the racial memory of the folk to early Christian clerical defection to the magical powers of the Druidic cults Christianity had supposedly subdued and replaced: the gods of the Druid world still had power denied to the prayer of the Christian priest. So says this belief. And there are many others.

Individually, the folk mind can be frustrating and fascinating at once. I see it in terms of several images: a grey dour block of untrimmed granite to be split into decipherable slabs by metaphorical verbal chisels which may be sharpened only by the acumen of seizing opportunity as one assesses the nature of the mind one is dealing with. Weeks and months of constant or desultory chippings may be required before the block begins to split and impart its hidden secrets: sometimes it stays intractable for ever.

Or like a wild bees' nest: the probings as delicate as a surgeon's fingers; the initial stings of rebuttal and denial of information; the indignant or ridiculed disavowal of knowledge of such information; the buzzing sallies one endures or evades – until the first layer of inhibiting wax is reached. A journalist need not worry about such sensitive approach: he will be gone in an hour: the folklore collector knows he has to spend months, even years with one mind. So melt the wax around the wild honey with sympathy and patience and with questions framed in confidential conversational form based on a knowledge of the working of the mind – and the honey begins to flow. Stay with the flow lest it seal again. Check and counter-check for confirmation – and more detail – without betraying by as much as a hint the source of the original information. And always remembering (in exculpation of our doubting friends) that people do not really know what they know until the recesses of their memories had been worked on in terms of that block of granite or the wild bees' nest. Any collector can confirm all that.

Whether I exaggerated my approach or not with excessive caution it is a fact that I could have avoided much of the inconvenience and minor hardship of our settling in at Glenhull had I definitely known on the day of my first visit that I would go to live there with my family, and not myself alone. But I didn't know. I am also a very shy man. Any of the neighbours would have had the place ready. This, however, is hindsight. They didn't know me; and I didn't know that some of my predecessors as tenants in 'The Bungalow' had arrived much as we had, apparently not the kind people you wish to associate with as neighbours in the usual sense. We weren't in Glenhull a week before, unwittingly, we gave reason for the people to believe I represented the worst character yet to arrive out of the blue.

6 Glenhull

The next morning came in light rain. A mist bank roofed Glenhull. I thought I could actually feel in this place more resentment – even hostility – than I had known elsewhere and as usual felt dismay, defeat. A day would come, however, when I would regard Glenhull as a green inkwell in the misshapen desks of the foothills of the Sperrins, myself an exhausted and bent nib trying to record even more of its story than I was doing. I was in Glenhull for two years and then, as far as I knew, back to free-lance writing and personal folklore-collecting in South Armagh. It would be to my future benefit to collect as much as I could. And I was testing out the theory of integration as a formula for success.

Glenhull was really an irregular basin divided by the meandering Owenkillew and bounded by low, peat-crested heights. To the west and north Coneyglen opened in shrubbery. Further on, severe and steep,

Glenlark, one of the wildest glens ever I've seen ending in mountain heath. A curtain of rain the colour of slow-blown ash usually blotted it out.

Scholar and traditionalist were to argue over the meaning of Glenhull itself. It would be related to one 'Cull' or MacCullagh. Tradition bearers would refute this and re-affirm in folk account and interpretation of phonetic Gaelic that it referred to the 'over' or last glen to be settled in one of the asides of Plantation clearance. It was O'Neill and Linney or McAlliney country: O'Neill trained his swordsmen in Coneyglen with the *batha-scors* or blackthorn sticks. Whatever the conflict, there was no doubt at all that Glenhull was the heart of an almost forgotten Folk Kingdom as valid as the Ring of Kerry, more valid perhaps than the Kingdom of Mourne. Proudly referred to in English as Munterloney (in Gaelic: Muintir Lionigh) and comprising several parishes as well as parts of others it was an area of ancient territorial lineage. Its great rival was the contiguous territory of Termonamguirk, with Carrickmore as its capital if such a term may be used. Rivalry between the two used once to be keen and serious. In those years of the early 1950s both still retained native Gaelic speakers, the greater number being in Munterloney.

On that first morning I knew none of those flecks of history and background. There were chores to be done before trying to rationalise feelings and impressions, or to reflect on why I was in Glenhull in the first place.

7 Meeting the People

The room chimney defied efforts to clear it and I would need a ladder. I would, Alice reminded me, need lime for temporary treatment of the gouged spaces in the plaster on the walls. And they would need water and more water. (Which reminded me of the folk-tale of the uncouth over-curious husband and how the 'Handy Woman' kept him out of the room where his wife was in labour. The 'Handy Woman' kept him on a constant trot for buckets of water, which she emptied out of a back window as he brought them in and told him to bring more: so that when next he heard of a confinement he remarked that 'God might look down on the one that has to carry the water'.)

There was a rusty pump in a soggy bank of rushes opposite the back door. It wouldn't work. Nor could I find a spring well. A piece of galvanised spouting stuck into the mountain stream which gushed close to the gable provided enough elevation to fill a bucket, brown and spate-stained. At Slieve Gullion in South Armagh no one would have dared use any stream water for drinking or food preparation. It was a week before I found a small well about a quarter of a mile away, but little used: the people used mountain streams such as the one at 'The Bungalow.'

In varying degrees of worry and panic I was apprehensive about the whole venture since it involved my wife and young family and my very placid niece Brigid O'Hare. But I was told not to worry. Look for lime. I went to look.

All the houses in Glenhull, except a few on the holms near the river, were situated at the top of long loanans or lanes with connecting lanes linking house to house. I went up the first lane closest to 'The Bungalow'. It was rudely and roughly surfaced with river stones, guttery and swimming with water. I saw a small house of room and kitchen with an open half-door and waited for the charge of a dog. None came.

Every one of my innate parochial inhibitions in approaching strangers naturally began to jostle; but before I could arrange – however self-consciously – a casual line of opening in appropriate vernacular – South Armagh style – a woman appeared. She was small, aged and rotund, with a plump face, and wearing wire-rimmed spectacles and a handkerchief on her head in familiar manner knotted under the chin. She came so swiftly to the door that I guessed she must have suddenly seen my approach; for instead of leaning over her half-door as was usual she opened it and skipped out into the street with remarkable agility, well away from the threshold. In the street, or yard, she was now in a position to cry for help if necessary! Her expression was stiff with suspicion, alarm and caution.

After my efforts at nest-clearing, the rain and the soot, and still unshaven and in old clothes, I looked more disreputable, I expect, than any hard-necked Tinker or Travelling Man with a bold western brogue, types she had had to deal with all her life. That was how I first met Anne McCrae, a native Gaelic speaker, a woman loaded with tradition in all shades of strength and delicacy in terms of social and human life material.

I sensed as well as saw her alarm, told her who I was and what I was; but the name 'folklore' and even 'Folklore Commission in Dublin' didn't appear to convey anything, or else she took my talk for just another lying line of blarney. When I added that I was living in the house below she showed genuine surprise: although related by marriage to my landlord Dan McCrae in Omagh even she did not seem to have been aware of our pending arrival in Glenhull: after all, as my landlord had strong doubts of my nationality and my going to live there anyhow he may have thought it discreet not to let anyone else know either. Omagh was twenty miles away.

We talked. She was monosyllabic, still cautious, resentful, her voice a whisper. I did not know that she lived alone (did not know either of those inter-connecting lanes between the houses); did not know that our South Armagh accent was to be classified with the so-called 'brogue' of the western peoples and the Travelling Men and Women.

She asked had I any children. I confirmed, gave their ages, said my wife would call on her; she instinctively murmured something about 'being welcome'. I should have added that I also had my niece with me: because in the next few days I almost set off rumours of scandalously immoral living which far out-stepped the alleged misdemeanours of some of the tenants who had preceded me in 'The Bungalow.'

I told her I wanted to buy lime. None could be bought but I was advised to try a house on the hillside across from her own: she did not tell me about that short inter-connecting lane and let me return the way I had come.

There was some building going on at the house up the lane I had been directed to. To a youngish lean-faced man who stared at me with caution and annoyance and justifiable suspicion, I told my errand. He had no lime to sell but would give me a bucketful. I thanked him, said I would return his bucket immediately, but he told me that later would do.

He was Malachi McAleer – known later to us all as 'Mal'. We often laughed over that first meeting, though he would never agree that he felt towards me as I have written, nor would I ever admit to the turmoil of shyness within me. Not once it seems had I explained why I had come to Glenhull, though if I had no one could blame people for hesitating to believe me just then. Mal's father was a native-speaker and storyteller, with a remarkably forthright mind on things folk and contemporary in all social norms. An uncle had been a school-master who had done some collection of minor traditions in the parish. So this family would have understood.

I returned the bucket immediately but he was not to be seen. I wanted to ask about the location of a well.

With temporary white-washing done, the furniture shrouded in newspapers and sacks, dusk was down. We had got used to the rush of the stream outside the gable, were already stepping habitually into the shallowest parts of pools outside the back door, could almost ignore the sound or *suuh* of the *Karrey,* the weir in the Owenkillew which diverted water to the race of the mill in Glenhull.

Our oil-lamp had a glass bowl and two wicks: paraffin gas lamps were only innovations then. The blinds cut off the presence of a countryside as yet unfriendly. Window lights like staring curious eyes without warmth or personality – as yet – shone from places in holm and on height where we could not suspect a house to have been. What our light meant to those houses we could easily guess – glorified tinkers at least, typical denizens of this abode; but while our predecessors could be traced to a neighbouring or distant townland or village we were completely unknown, our entry unmarked, unannounced. We might have been moonlight flitters chased out of Connacht.

After a meal and a wash and a clean up something like controlled disorder reigned in the kitchen: beds had to be dismantled and put up each night. But there was nevertheless a feeling of some content and relaxation and ease.

Until we had our first visitor within an hour.

'Any men in this house?'

Alice was breast-feeding Peter: sitting in an old low armchair I was undressing Michael. When the peremptory knock sounded Brigid O'Hare went into the passageway to the front door which was out of our sight anyway.

'Any men in this house?' the man's voice repeated as she opened the door. The words though clipped in the Northern accent had an intonation or overlay of American, as I thought. What now I wondered?

Before I could formulate thought, theory or fear the man was standing over me where I sat, having pushed in ahead of Brigid without invitation or explanation. He was lightly-built, thin-faced, wore urban style clothes with heavy overcoat, scarf and a hat which he hadn't removed.

He kept his hands in his overcoat pockets as he talked down at me, his accent still puzzling, even unintelligible. Then he asked:

'Have you worked in land?'

I said I had.

In a manner which he, no doubt, assumed to be so polite as to be authoritative he says:

'I'm looking for a man. Help is pretty scarce here, so I thought I'd be first in. You can start right away in the morning.' He gave me no chance to interrupt. 'You did say you've worked in land. I have a road to make first of all ... ' He went on to tell the name of the tenant who had preceded me, the name of the man before him; and then I wondered why he felt I should be interested.

His initial manner had so annoyed me that I deliberately parried other questions with equivocal answers. I thought I had this character in his group alright. His affected accent annoyed me even more: in an area of heavy emigration the Irish-American sound was never too unusual, but it could be irritating when it was overbearing. This one was.

And neither Alice nor Brigid O'Hare, standing all the time at the thin-boarded door between the kitchen and the passageway, interjected by word or look that I should – or they would – end this interlude.

I told the fellow I was sorry I could not oblige him; told him what I was and why I was where I was and who had sent me – and then was thoroughly sorry I said it as I had, or had let his garrulous tongue carry him so far. He would be near the fifties perhaps. He sat down as if felled, rose immediately as if from an ejector seat, removed his hat, sat again. He kept rising and sitting and trying to talk, then was stammering apologies. He got up again and immediately apologised to Alice and to Brigid O'Hare. He gaped at me, I told him to sit down and forget about it all.

He wasn't wholly to blame. Certainly he was precipitous, while I must have looked like someone glad to welcome work of any kind. Rumour about my contacts with the people had, of course, already sped around the glen; a man could hardly be blamed for deducing that here was another fugitive glad of a haven and work.

We persuaded the man to stay for a cup of tea. I deliberately used folk vernacular to banish his embarrassment. He talked; mentioned a rare event to come, a dance in a school in a townland called Crock. I knew he was worried about possible local reaction in gossip to his blunder. When he left I saw him to the road. He apologised repeatedly and profusely and begged me not to mention the incident to anyone, as I knew he would.

Until now I never have.

8 The Quest Begins

Within two days of arriving in Glenhull I met three men who were to take a notable place in the success of my quest for folklore: Francis McBride, a neighbour; Michael Morris of Carnanransy, and Francis McAleer of Muninameale. A fourth man, in some ways the most outstanding character I ever met, Padraig McCullagh of Curraghinalt, was not to appear until later. He lived in the adjoining parish of Rousky, while the others were parishioners of Greencastle which included Glenhull.

I met McBride when I went to borrow a ladder to clear the room chimney. With a handshake he welcomed me to 'this part of the world', said he was using the ladder just then but that he would bring it along himself and clear the chimney for me, which he did in a day or so. (I wondered over the renovations in houses in the townland and learned later that people who believed their houses might be selected as the venue for the religious custom of 'The Stations' due in March were getting prepared. Only a faint folk memory of this custom existed at Slieve Gullion.)

McBride introduced me to his family. When I explained why I was in Glenhull he believed there 'might be some folklore left' but regretted that the collection had been left so late and added: 'If only you hada been here even last year. There was an old man in Crock could have filled a book himself . . . '

I did not mention that one is always too late everywhere, that one hears that same phrase used; but that people do not realise themselves what they know and retain until a collector has gone to work with them.

McBride was a man of medium height, in his late fifties, lithe and lightly built. His face was thin and, though hollowed, fresh enough, with a high nose and grey pleasant eyes hiding a mischievous glint of humour. He wore a cloth cap in the old fashion with the peak fastener unbuttoned, the peak itself drawn forward over the forehead and eyes.

In the shelter of a stack of fodder pulled into the shape of a huge mushroom we talked. He would give me all the help he could. But he had work to do, which I understood, mentioning that I had worked on farms; and that any way (and here was a deliberate throwaway of a vernacular bait) that the air was still too thin, the day with the *kaar* of winter about it. ('Kaar' – in phonetics – meant to grimace in sarcasm, resentment or wry bitterness.) He asked 'had we that word too' and told a story: the first piece of Community lore I picked up in Glenhull.

He pointed to a house and said that a man who once lived there had quarreled with a relative and was ordered never to 'set foot in the house again whether I'm alive or dead'. The relative retorted that he would call when the other was dead and lay a fist under his nose. 'If you do,' cries the old man, 'I'll rise and strike you.' The old man died and the relative was seen going to the 'wake house'. Asked if he had carried out his threat he said he had and was then asked if the man had 'made shape to rise?'

'No,' he replied, 'but he kind of *kaared*.'

I was to learn more about McBride's highly developed sense of humour from other narrators later on.

Before leaving he told me I should see about buying a supply of turf and added:

'I might be able to spare you a little, but not enough.' (Turf cutting had died out at Slieve Gullion.) 'We only cut what does us for the year. The winter after Christmas here can be bad, and no coal lorry will ever get through from Derry. I'll find out where you might be fit to get a wee clamp to be going on with.'

Back in the house I found that Brigid O'Hare had been to Frank Morris' shop, had explained who and what I was but without making clear the family relationship. Frank had a namesake and would ask the man to call as soon as possible. Michael Morris of Carnanransy called, in fact, within an hour.

Michael arrived while I was white-washing in the room where we proposed to sleep once that chimney had been cleared. I saw him through the window: maybe in his mid-forties and active, well-built, regular features looking serious, intense and intelligent. I reached the open front door just as he knocked. He introduced himself, the voice in good expression, rich in vowel sound, the intonation soft, confident, warm and sincere.

He was in a hurry but had heard about me in the ship. He would be glad to help; if I was agreeable he would bring some people to see me. He declined to come in, no doubt deducing that we were in disarray in making a long uninhabited house at least presentable and running into unforeseen troubles. I have the impression still that Michael Morris scarcely 'halted on his foot', (I was in old clothes suitable for white-washing) kept up a pace in his talk and brief exchange and more hurriedly still sped from our gate on a bicycle as if he were a man feeling rebuffed.

I glanced at Glenhull. The mist had lifted. I recalled South Armagh. Amid the circle of hills around Slieve Gullion the undulating valley of Dromintee could breathe a living sense of quietue like the vibrant peace to be found in the ruins of a monastic cloister, the roofless walls absorbed with the same reality of silence as the ring of hills around Slieve Gullion.

In Glenhull the sense of loneliness might have been that of an ageing spirit of the mythic herd worn by flight, too weary to continue towards the era of evolving community somewhere beyond the rim of the peat-crested hilltops.

Epitomising that image of flight and abandonment were the telegraph poles from Glenhull to Greencastle and Omagh, rising in outline against the skyline before disappearing down the far side.

'Glenhull?' said a young Post Office engineer to me in Omagh. 'Glenhull is the first place to be cut off in any snow storm. You'll see.'

9   An Able Storyteller

I was cycling to Greencastle next day when I first met Francis McAleer outside his home in Muninameale. He stood smoking a wooden pipe at the end of his loanan – unusually wide and gateless, as to a forge: the house itself was low, long and entirely thatched, with buttresses back and front propping weak spots in the walls: the oldest house they said in the district.

A long hill had to be walked from Glenhull to the top in Muninameale near a bridge known as The Nine Pipes. He watched me ride up and spoke a polite though stiff word of greeting to which I replied as I rode on; I was anxious about a supply of coal in Eddie MacCullagh's at Greencastle, three miles from our place. Yet I got the impression that McAleer had been watching and waiting. Our house in Glenhull lay directly below his own across the river like a grey cob of a pebble from a dried-up river, with the back of the hillside rising from its gradual climb through ditched-off fields and white washed houses into the carpet of peat of the 'Moss' or turf-lands at the foot of Oughminacrory Hill. Far beyond rose the peaks of Sawel and Dart, matronly mountains in the Sperrin range proper, usually with berets of cloud. Here and there in the far-flung landscape, glens cut by rivers showed like the chopping-strokes of a fabulous axeman in a folk-tale.

Returning from Greencastle half-an-hour later Francis Daniel, as he was popularly called, still lingered on the road. I was now convinced he had been watching and waiting. I knew that almost any unusual movement in a countryside of a local, let alone a stranger, could be interpreted with uncanny accuracy. I knew that every word I had said, what had been said to me, had been the topic of gossip and deduction and related to every move and journey I made, such as this chore in search of fuel.

His greeting this time was less taut and suspicious and he added 'Sir' to it. I got off the bike. We spoke of the weather, the proximity of Christmas and so on. Next he asked me was I the man who had 'likely taken Dan McCrae's place?' He welcomed me with a hand-shake. Then said: 'If it's not too bold to ask, sir, what business do you follow?' I told him; giving the usual vernacular explanation – old cracks and talk from the fireside and all that. Other questions followed, among carefully set interlinking gossip. He was dubious and suspicious about me, my family, everything in my work and in my accent. Not once did he reply to my explanation about folklore.

He was a man in his early sixties and owned 'a small farm of twenty-two acres'. (At Slieve Gullion in those years this acreage would have set him among the very few 'big' farmers.) Below medium height and firmly built, his voice was low, careful but clear, by no means suggesting exceptional range or vocal ability in characterisation. The face was pale with the skin drawn tightly over the bones and nose; not a countenance hinting of talents like high mental gifts of imagination and memory. He, too, wore his cap drawn forward over his forehead. His eyes were dark and restless, always searching me as if in doubt when I flicked a glance at him: like a man suspecting a leg-pull deceit: there was that social repercussion of derision or scorn to be avoided if it were. After all he had never seen me before in his life.

I did not know it that December morning in Muninameale by the roadside; but I was talking to one of the ablest folk storytellers I have ever met in twenty-five years work of collecting in old Ulster and the bordering counties. Days and nights ahead I would marvel at the transformed mobility of those taut features, the shift of expression in the voice, the amazing memory, the vivid characterisation in intonation and dialogue: the very countenance now so stiff would even make comment with smile or flash of eye that could vanish just as quickly, till the man's entire personality seemed to undergo change according to the mood and tempo of the story or character whose words he could mimic.

Suddenly he stopped, turned, and looked in silence down at our house far below across the Owenkillew. Just as suddenly he said that his wife was ill or he would invite me into his house, told me about his family at home and in England, suddenly stopped again, considered, and while staring down at the road looked up sharply as he shot at me:

'And you tell me it's old rehearsals you're after . . . ?'

I had never heard folk-tales or folklore referred to as 'rehearsals' until then: an almost perfect definition of the nature of all oral lore. He went on:

'I used to listen here to an old man called MacCrory at old rehearsals – he told them in Irish as well as English. I knew no English myself till after I went to school. So I doubt if I could be of any service to you, sir; my stories might not be very good. It's thirty years since I heard Netchy' – this was MacRory's nickname – 'at the rehearsals – me and a son of old Annie McCrae's beside you over there. You'll be very welcome to call here. And maybe I might call with you.'

He next mentioned, off-hand, that he heard I 'could do with a load or two of turf'. He would oblige me and Francis McBride's son 'Francis Henry or Francis Frank Jack's son Mal' would cart them home for me. He mentioned himself that he would be better known as Francis Daniel: this use of the Christian names of oneself, father, grandfather or grandmother was Gaelic, of course; it had survived at Slieve Gullion in a two-named form and erroneously termed a nickname.

Frankly, I had little hope or feeling at that first meeting that the man was telling no lie: that his 'rehearsals' could hardly be of any value: he did not seem to have the mind. I was either dense, stupid, otherwise too worried or dull.

Francis Daniel was, in fact, an artist. Before I was to leave Glenhull he would epitomise in himself, his house and his people the triumph and tragedy of the vanishing folk scene. (He was the first man to record for the BBC in Belfast their first full-length folk-tale, 'Old Lord Erin's Son', told without hesitation, embarrassment or inhibition in a studio, myself facing him for an audience; told in all its risque detail as if sitting at a Glenhull fireside.)

10 Reds in Glenhull

Francis McBride dutifully came and 'redd' the room chimney of accumulated nests. (Coming from Confession people would ask quite seriously: 'Did you get redd?' – of one's sins by Absolution.) I no longer had a head for heights and was more than grateful to him. He didn't surprise me when, hesitantly, he revealed he was aware of almost every move I had made and of people I had met. He came in, but was very shy, removing his cap. As I was also expected to compile a glossary of Anglo-Irish idiomatic speech his own vernacular intrigued me. Working on the chimney he had remarked that 'it was wild cold'. (Later, there was to be the boy who used this superlative in a superlative way when he said he had a pigeon that was 'wild tame.') 'Almost' truncated itself to 'a' most' and when beginning on a task he 'joined to do it'. 'Vexed' retained the Elizabethan derivation, and did not denote anger but the opposite – sadness or contrition. *'Suuh'* or sound of the *Karrey* or weir was then new to me, mentioned in connection with a weather omen: I had already 'joined to start' my glossary of idioms and expressions in Anglo-Irish speech.

I had no intention to begin collecting in earnest until the people had properly got to know me: but on that day there was one interlude which involved the popular equation of folklore with Fairies. In Tyrone these were 'Wee folk'. ('Wee people' at Slieve Gullion: 'Gentry' in other places and 'Good Neighbours' in Mourne: all terms of superstitious flattery designed to forestall any malicious or capricious intentions on the part of the invisible host – with good supernatural hearing.)

McBride went singularly quiet when this topic came up, and I wondered which inhibition was hardening like a lava over his lively and loquacious personality: fear of being thought simple-minded, naive; fear of making himself ridiculous or being ridiculed by neighbours should I relate my source? All this was a familiar mental labyrinth which I had trod warily with people elsewhere, even at Slieve Gullion. 'No,' said the old man, 'I don't believe in the Wee People but they're there just the same.' And Lone Whitethorn Bushes all over the land testify to the lingering respect.

But when he asked was not such belief superstition I had an inkling as to what was wrong. A priest in the parish, as priests had done elsewhere, had denounced all folk belief as being superstitious; but in Greencastle there had been practical as well as theological (however wrong-headed) sound cause. A man who sincerely believed that his wife had not actually died a normal death but had been abducted in childbirth by the fairies – who leave a substitute body in place of the other – persuaded two friends to help dig up the corpse; he hoped to decide one way or the other if the remains were really those of his wife. The priest accidentally came upon them opening the grave, heard the reason, and wielded his blackthorn stick in understandable fury. He later preached on the matter.

(A few remarks on that belief: Again the racial memory is at work on facts rooted in ancient pre-Christian history. If the incomers really did over-run and burn the souterrain builders and their forts without having knowledge of such underground constructions, the builders would take refuge to elude this early scorched-earth policy of the invader. Living underground, pregnant women and male children were kidnapped in attempts to restore the vigour of their own race.)

To dismiss the matter of the local instance of this belief McBride referred to a dance in Crock that night. Brigid O'Hare was eager to see what a dance would be like in such a remote area. So indeed was I. After all, in the Post Office with its gloomy grille of close wooden laths no customer went inside while another was being served but, like penitents at Confession, patiently waited until the other came out.

The school in Crock was small and white-washed. Desks had been moved along the walls to provide seating and the music was supplied by a simple melodeon.

The dances were mixed, Irish reels, fox-trots and waltzes. While never a dancer I could usually 'pass myself' at such affairs and Brigid and I took a few turns on the floor; very much aware that every eye was on us. The local curate was there in hat and overcoat standing near the door. There was nothing of interest, traditional or otherwise, for me to note. I talked with a few people, found them friendly without being over affable, and after about an hour we left for home.

On the following Sunday Brigid and I went to Mass in Greencastle; Alice still refused to go out until she had cleaned and arranged things in the house to her satisfaction, and, of course, Peter was an infant.

Greencastle Church was a plain unpretentious building, weather and time darkened, with a small bell-tower at one gable. On the roadside opposite the gate men and boys stood talking and smoking, just as I would have done in South Armagh, until the last bell announced that Mass was about to begin. As in Dromintee, no women stood outside: and as in Dromintee the sexes did not mix, each went to their own aisle: 'men's aisle' and 'women's aisle', although the positioning was opposite to that observed in South Armagh. I noticed that the inscriptions on the Stations of the Cross were written in Gaelic.

Mass began. When the congregation sat up to hear instruction and sermon I noticed the glances shot at me: Brigid had obediently gone to the 'women's aisle'; I saw glances being shot at her as well.

He was a young, impulsive-minded curate and his subject was Communist infiltration into the Ireland of the day: particularly rural Ireland.

The priest claimed that Communism had already established itself in 'cells' in every county in Ireland: 'Perhaps in every parish. They have agents on the move organising everywhere.' He said that in fact there were Communists who were Irishmen and Irish women: added that 'some of them may even be here with us right now.' Whether he meant in the parish or in the church I do not know: but I knew I was more than uneasy. I could almost *feel* the eyes upon Brigid and myself. The concept of my very devout niece being suspected of Communist intentions should perhaps have amused me. But no such idea crossed my mind, because the priest went on to explain the Communist technique of infiltration. He said they would 'go to Mass – even receive Holy Communion' perform every religious duty and obligation; they would not 'openly preach Communism.' First of all they would 'slowly gain the confidence of the people' and then 'slowly undermine the Faith.' And so on.

At home Alice and Brigid laughed. Then I wondered. Suppose people took the instruction literally? I could, of course, see the priest and explain and get him to make an announcement. But I learned discreetly he was a man totally indifferent, indeed opposed 'as paganism' to all folk belief in any form. Furthermore, I knew enough of the reactions of the collective rural mind to realise that any such public disclaimer could rebound and arouse the wrong sort of attention: because I *wanted* to infiltrate into the local collective mind in my own time, in my own manner. I knew that the people – however much the statement may amuse or rise hackles on some clerics – resented the clergy as an aid to my type of inquiry. 'Leave old thorns and priests alone,' ran the adage. 'Give them their dues and leave them alone.' I would be put in a category outside the kinship of their hearth, heart, confidence and memory: as if I were a teacher, a doctor or someone in that social class.

I was perturbed; and would have been thoroughly alarmed had I known what the people were saying and thinking about us as tenants of 'The Bungalow.' I met Francis Daniel on the road near his home next day and he said stiffly to me:

'How did you and your wife enjoy the dance in Crock?'

With the priest's sermon in my mind I must have been so flabbergasted that I hardly replied. If such an assumption had got around the district what would people think of the 'two-woman man in the Bungalow' except that such promiscuity was taken to be standing practice with any Communist: especially when it could be said that 'my wife' went off to a dance in a strange school with me while we left three young children alone in a strange house to fend for themselves!

We had no more visitors, but I took the two eldest boys up to old Anne McCrae. They got on fine. No child, no matter how often it came in, was ever allowed out of a house in Glenhull without a biscuit, sweet or, failing either, a lick of a damp spoon dipped in sugar; a custom backed again by Fairy belief. Annie said not a word about us and the dance, the priest's sermon or my niece.

I had work to do indoors making and installing cupboards. A week later a man named Patrick Bradley called on me. He said simply:

'You were at the dance in Crock. But I now hear a good char-ack-ter of you. You're a decent married man with a wife an' family an' you have a niece staying with you.'

So they had been talking.

11 Padraig McCullagh of Curraghinalt: Craftsman

Brigid O'Hare left Glenhull for home in South Armagh before Christmas week, although she offered to stay if we wished. Valiantly and without one word of complaint she had already done more than even such a gentle soul could be expected to endure – even without silence – especially for Alice and the children. The weather was getting worse. When the glen came up soundly white one morning she decided she had better go – while she could.

There were temporary chores for me to do inside and outside the house: the pathway needed attention, and around the walls the walk needed a pitching of stones and gravel to throw off the water which lay in pools. I had my eye on a swamp which, when drained, might make a vegetable garden: I had made gardens before with pick and shovel out of haggards of buried stones. But only channels could be cut as yet. Pitching of the pathways would have to wait until Spring.

People were meanwhile getting to know me. A man would stop now and exchange a few words, though still revealing uncertainty about me and my job. (I recalled the first vagabond venture with an ash-plant in the Mournes. Outside Hilltown a man called to me one day of snow. He had seen me 'knocking about'. Was it true that my job was as I said it was? Folklore-collecting? Not debt collecting? Then what was folklore? And was I getting paid for doing that? Was I sure now I wasn't an inspector of some kind – or an IRA man on the run? Not even a clerk on the run, after dabbling in the till of some mythical employer? Or a broken-down schoolmaster? I could assure him I was none of the types he had enumerated. Then I must have money behind me? No? I had been a half-a-crown a day farm worker and freelance writer until now· Well, he had been over a good part of the world from Butte in Montana (where the Mourne folk emigrate) to Tasmania in a sailing ship, had seen all sorts of queer jobs, but I was the first he met to make a living out of the bluddy fairies.

I was getting flecks of lore, arranging my approach. My typewriter was fifty years of age; and one day a man dashed into the house out of a downpour, saw me at work in the kitchen and wanted to know 'what kind of a machine that was and what was it for?' Around Glenhull I was to meet a few comparatively young men who had never seen a train, though eighty percent of the old people had spent at least six years as emigrants in the United States.

Michael Morris and Francis McBride called one night. The atmosphere was careful and formal, and neither had yet started to use my Christian name: until they would I would not begin really to work. (A former workpal of mine, Paddy the Racker, had a relative axiom when he went as a servant-man from the Hiring Ground of Newry: he said that he remained on in any place, or farm, until the 'cat and the dog really got to know him; then it was time to shift.')

Morris was a man with confident opinions, knew his own mind, respected the thing folk as well as contemporary event. He, too, had spent some years as a counter-hand in a big store in New York, had also worked at various jobs in London, but liked his home place intensely. McBride had never emigrated. He seemed tongue-tied because he was uncertain to indulge his sense of impish humour.

Morris finally mentioned that he had been in touch with Padraig McCullagh or 'Padraig Phelimy Laidir' as they called him. All spoke Gaelic, McBride diffidently. (I was delighted to notice, however, that while he had removed his cap, as Morris had his hat, when they came in, he had since replaced it, becoming more at ease.) McCullagh was to be brought to me: it would be too difficult to try to find the man himself; he worked two farms on each side of a hill and might be anywhere.

No one then even suspected that the man had such knowledge of craftsmanship as he was to reveal later.

Padraig McCullagh came to our house for the first time one night in the following January of 1950. It could be said that he literally ran in.

The meeting had finally been arranged by Michael Morris. In the weeks between, my new-found friends called now and then, all usually with gifts of eggs or potatoes or a fowl, even a few sacks of turf when our own supply had not been delivered. I had been out and about, meeting people, talking, inquiring about blacksmiths' forges and cobblers' shops and such centres of talk and ceili. But the dead and vacant forges were already becoming a symbol of the dwindling vigour of the folk mind.

That day, however, everyone seemed to have heard of a 'great ceili' to be held in our house that night. There was even some talk about 'invitations'. I did not know until I returned that Padraig McCullagh was due. I did not miss among some of the younger people a tone of amusement, even the supercilious in what they assumed to be the enlightened attitude to observe to anything even dimly connected with the thing 'folk'.

Francis McBride and Mal McAleer were first to arrive. Two strange men followed and were introduced. All removed their caps, then replaced them quietly later. Talk was stiff and langled. McBride talked about Christmas to one of the men: how did he 'get it over him', and told the usual anecdote. A local man over-fond of his bottle, and with his debt 'on the slate' in every pub, found himself at Christmas unable to borrow a cent in drink, and was blankly refused till he would 'wipe the slate clean.' Asked at Christmas morning Mass how he had spent Christmas he replied: 'Quiet and holy – as it should be spent'.

Francis Daniel came next, his first visit, with two other strangers. Courteous in a formal traditional way he sounded self-consciously pompous as he shook Alice's hand, then mine, bidding us both welcome to Glenhull, hoped we would be happy, said that the neighbours were good and agreeable (as indeed they were and more) and then said the exact same phrases to me. He also shook hands with the children. He was wearing a heavy overcoat which he declined to remove, walked the length of the long narrow kitchen, and sat on a distant chair back from the other men. At the time, of course, I did not know he was such a storyteller as he later proved himself to be. He sat like a man who, having performed a ritualistic duty, wanted to remain unnoticed. He spoke little, looked preoccupied, more cautious still than puzzled.

By then I was uneasy myself. What, I wondered, was expected of me? I had the notion they expected long, serious, weighty talk on the 'history of the place', learned statement on folklore and all that. Because, how or why I do not know – I was being referred to as 'The folklore man in the Bungalow from University College in Dublin.' The Folklore Commission had been located in rooms in the college certainly.

Others came in, including some young men. One was Frank Morris of Crockanboy. Unable to wait he stood at the door; he had brought me names of people to call on. He was hatless, a young man with an engaging countenance, brilliant dark eyes behind horn-rimmed spectacles and with excellent teeth. Frank Morris mentioned that I was being talked about in Gortin, our nearest wee town over ten miles away, and Newtownstewart, as well as in The Cross and Ballinascreen, the old name they used for Draperstown. I suddenly had the impression of a countryside in a whirl with speculation, amusement or plain derision.

Frank Morris, though in a hurry, said he would nevertheless wait until Padraig McCullagh had arrived: this was the first intimation I got of the genuine esteem in which people of his type held the great traditionalist.

(Frank Morris, quiet and gentle voiced, was a determined Republican and had spent a term in Crumlin Road for his beliefs and activities. On Easter Sunday outside Greencastle Church I would see him rebuke his curate vehemently though courteously in legitimate objection to the manner in which the curate had impetuously snatched a Tricolour held by one of Morris' colleagues. Morris had simply been reading The Proclamation of the Easter Rising.)

The house was now full of men. The fire burned well with coal and turf. We had discovered a serious blow-down but it seemed to behave itself for this occasion; it could get so bad that, no matter what the weather, the door had to be propped open to prevent us being kippered. There was still no sign of McCullagh, nor had Michael Morris shown up. The men prevented Alice from rising to make tea.

In this bit of commotion there was a noise at the back door like a hand erratically scratching in search of a latch. Alice, on her feet, turned to go and see who or what it was. The hand by then had found the latch and, as if being pursued, opened the door, left it open and the sound of heavy boots beat on the concrete to the door to the kitchen from the passageway. The man (as Alice later told me) opened the door just as she reached it and charged past her without a word. Not since we had come to the house had any visitor used the back door.

The man hurried in a crouch into the crowded kitchen before anyone fully realised he was among them. In his run he had clawed an old grey cap from his head, wheeled this way and that in search of a seat like a scholar late for school and expecting rebuke while hoping to elude it. His head came up as quickly as a cat's, then down, as Alice came in again. He flicked a similar glance at me, found the corner of a chair, ignored it, and instead squatted where he was with his back to us, trying to make talk to some man near him. I hadn't a notion who he was but I was soon aware of the odd silence which slowly settled on the kitchen.

No one spoke. Everyone seemed to be preplexed, then embarrassed: as if some unwritten code had been ignored and broken. They were, of course, waiting for the man to rise and perform the ritual little ceremony of traditional welcome. But he remained where he was, crushing his cap in powerful hands or wiping one of the hands swiftly across his close-cropped grey head and red face.

I saw that the man was shy. Then I rose with the intention of welcoming him, to put him at ease. Alice was nearer to him, understood what was in my mind, gave me a significant glance and I stayed where I was. The others still maintained silence, but their glances went askance from the man to us.

Francis McBride quietly rose from the armchair nearest the fire (where, in fact, he had had to be coaxed to sit) and crossed to the newcomer with his hand out. In a voice too hushed and solemn for Francis he said:

'How are you Patrick Phelimy . . . ?'

By then the newcomer had put on his cap, for others were wearing their own. He seemed to leap to his feet – though I noticed he was lame. He took McBride's hand. His face was flushed. McBride slowly, hesitantly returned to his chair. Someone else rose and shook hands with the man. He had squatted but was back on his feet again. He squatted once more. Then up on his feet again he limped noticeably as he thrust through the chairs towards me. His cap was off again, his hand out. His greeting was in Gaelic. The face burned with shyness, the grey eyes alive with excitement. His hand quivered with great nervous power. Then he spun, on his lame leg – gave the same handshake and greeting to Alice, and as an after-thought shook hands with the children, all the time speaking Gaelic gutturally. Finally he turned to look for the place he had vacated, seemed unable to identify it. And then something else happened.

Every man was on his feet, shaking his hand. Some of them returned his greeting in Gaelic also. From his corner in slow measured strides Francis Daniel came and welcomed the man. The man himself, speaking sometimes in English, sometimes in Gaelic, seemed to be genuinely surprised and moved by their obvious respect for him.

McBride had already left his chair and offered it to the man. 'The Chair of Pleasure,' he said with a quick, husky, short laugh. He refused it. Everyone offered him their seat. In the midst of it all Michael Morris came in, smiled, and said to the man: 'Oh, so you're there, Patrick Phelimy.' He too crossed the floor and shook hands and they exchanged greetings and banter in Gaelic.

That was how Padraig McCullagh – Padraig Phelimy Laidir – first came to our house in Glenhull.

So much had been said, so much expected from the man that somehow the expectations didn't seem possible just then. He was about five feet nine, the shoulders square and powerful. The face was also square and heavy, showing determination. He wore an old stained raincoat buttoned tight to his chin, the lower half swinging loose.

They talked in Gaelic for a time, McCullagh spinning or twirling on his chair to return the remarks from wherever they came. Everyone simply ignored Alice and me. I didn't know Gaelic – apart from a word or two anyway – and had never heard such conversation in the native tongue since my grandmother and other Old Age Pensioners in the 1920's in South Armagh used to converse outside her house every Friday, all smoking clay pipes taken from their breasts.

I did not know it that night in Glenhull, but that had been the first time in many years that such a group of men had got together.

The Gaelic ceased and the talk went on in English. I asked McCullagh to take off his raincoat, for he was uncomfortably warm as I could see. He laughed his short husky laugh and said, 'Like the landlord – Maybe I have no back to the one under it.'

'Like my shirt,' I said: a traditional rejoinder: at which Alice jestingly interpolated in mock reproachment something about me suggesting she was lazy and neglecting her own job. McCullagh enjoyed the little joke, suddenly stood up, hauled off his raincoat, rolled it into a ball before I could get near him, and flung it from him against the bottom of the partition towards the corner. He said nothing when Alice took it and hung it up on a coat-rack I had fitted up one side of the door inside the kitchen.

Some simple remark started it from Michael Morris. McCullagh, hand swiping his head and face, answered quickly in Gaelic, paused, repeated in English and went on. Folk tradition simply rolled from the man as oats come from a threshing mill: all in an easy, calm confidence, hardly touched by his excitement or the emotion of the events as he narrated them. His cap seemed to be on and off. I sat back and wrote as he talked. No one took the slightest notice of me: they were intent on McCullagh's words. I found I could probe systematically on any point without any fear of his withdrawing into himself. He was enjoying having listeners as they enjoyed listening.

He had been persuaded by McBride to sit in the armchair. But he rarely sat still in any one position for more than a minute. The lame leg perhaps troubled him, yet he kept heaving one leg across the other with hands locked behind the knee, and then would begin to spin, to paw his face, to swipe off his cap, to pull at one lock of sprouting hair in his fringe, then at the other, and then twist and spin back again until the arms of the chair stopped him. He even tried to make the chair spin. Not once did he stop talking tradition: not folktales, but material in Community and Historical categories. The cap while on his head was pulled until the peak leaned over one ear, then the other, then sat like a beret with the peak to the back.

Alice made tea and handed it round, but even then he didn't stop talking. I kept writing. The children were put to bed without noise. Some of the men left. McCullagh talked on. I wrote.

It was almost 3.00 in the morning before he rose to go. By then everyone else had gone. He punched his way into the old raincoat, saying it was only a nuisance anyway. He had come on a bicycle – without any light – and this he hauled from along the back wall and let it bounce in his hand down the steps to the road. I offered to lend him a lamp but he said he had been 'coming the road all his life' and didn't need a light.

I tried to fix up a future meeting – at his own house if he wished – but he replied at once that 'Micky John Katie' (as Michael Morris was known in familiar parlance) would let me know. He seemed to have become rather brusque so suddenly that I wondered if he had been disappointed and said so. His reply was as swift as rebuke.

'I'd go to the far end of the county on foot for a night like that in your school.' (The early Gaelic League had conducted night schools for a time in Greencastle).

Then he was gone on his bike into the darkness with a phrase in Gaelic floating back over his houlder. I went back into the house.

That peculiar sense of a vibrant vacancy which throbs with the echoes of good talk and merriment lingered in the kitchen. When Alice had gone to bed I sat and smoked and recalled it again. I remembered that McCullagh had not smoked: remembered too that I had neglected to bring up from the McCrae's pub any kind of refreshment. I continued to make notes of points I recalled from his talk, to etch something that would afford a guide to the man's real personality.

Then I had the queer sensation that he was unreal; that it had never happened; that I would never see him again.

That was Padraig McCullagh: blacksmith, cooper, saddler, shoemaker, brush-maker, skilled poteen-maker, craftsman in straw and rush, the latter unique: so unique that when he made a set for the National Museum his craftsmanship was exhibited at a British Association meeting in Dublin.

Later that month Sean O'Sullivan, archivist of the Folklore Commission, wrote to compliment me on an excellent collection. The credit fundamentally went to McCullagh, McBride and Michael Morris.

12 Collecting in Earnest

Before the end of that winter I was well established into the rhythm I had planned: collect during the night and type during the day, Saturday and Sunday included. There were occasional impediments, not least the smoking chimney which defied every trick and device to remedy. Our visitors stayed away; I later heard that despite our good fire of turf and coal they complained of being 'foundered' in Murphy's because of the door, propped open with a spade. Turf smoke, though it impregnates one's clothes, is bearable; coal smoke can be deadly, with its consequence of head-aches.

Rats had also invaded the area of our water supply and the fear of these getting in through the open door made another hazard. But these were lighter episodes. In the more philosophical and agreeable moods I wrote a short story about the smoking chimney. I broadcast it in the first person, attributing the smoke to the cutting of a Lone Fairy Thorn during a fuel scarcity in a snow storm, of which we already had had a few. The story got around as fact, not fiction, even as far as Canada: inquiries to the Tourist

Board about the Tyrone house where fairies smoked out the residents came as late as a few years back!

I had by then collected several tales and other traditions from Francis Daniel in his thatched house which, despite its age, looked so snug if squat under its heavy poll of thatch accumulated over the decades.

He lived with two daughters and a son and his wife: a gentle soul with one of the most delicately perfect complexions I have ever seen on a woman. One leg had been amputated and she moved about on crutches. Her usual seat was one side of the open fireside. None of the turf-burning houses had grates of any kind fitted to the hearths.

The entire kitchen was in an ancient traditional pattern, including the 'Cooltyee Bed' set in an outshot and, unlike others in the area, retaining the inner light walls built of small stone instead of wood, with inlets called 'Boles' to provide compartments for boot and clothes brushes and the like.

The first night I went in 'the great ceili' in our house was the main topic. Francis was absent.

A gramophone was played for my entertainment, the records being referred to as 'plates'. The mother would then rise – her exquisitely coloured countenance looking so fragile – and move to the room on her crutches. When Francis arrived, in overcoat and cap, he welcomed me a bit pompously, and stood listening to a tune, making critical remarks: he had once played in a local band. Then he took off his overcoat. At once his son got up and Francis took his chair. The girls took up knitting they had put aside as I went in. A silence fell.

I wondered why the woman had gone to the room; wondered if I were in the way. I learned later that she feared Francis would make a fool of himself before me with his tales. He asked me if I had got any 'old rehearsals' and knowing he meant folk-tales proper I said not yet. He accurately observed that none of the old stories had been told at our ceili; and went on to recall the man Netchy who 'talked just like Patrick Phelimy Laidir in your house, in Irish and then in English: Netchy had a feed-all bag of stories, a great boozer and a great mower and a pair of breasts on him like a woman.' (He had laid out the man's corpse.)

As he talked his personality seemed to thaw, to generate warmth and ease. Abruptly he got up, whispered to one of his daughters, then went to the room and after a while returned, not to the former chair, but to a long red-painted stool along the 'Cooltyee' from which the curtains had been drawn back to expose the bed itself. He still wore his cap. With his hands behind his head and leaning his elbows on the bed behind him he said he would try one of Netchy's 'old rehearsals.'

Again he warned me that it was thirty years since he had told the tale; told how he had heard it; how Netchy used to tell it in Gaelic, then in the English translation; and how he told sections of the tale only, one on each night.

'If me and Annie McCrae's son weren't fit to tell him where and how he had left off the night before he wouldn't tell us. He'd tell the same piece again.'

He slipped his pipe into his waistcoat pocket and waited: his wife returned from the room as quietly as a shadow and sat on her usual seat.

Only the clicking of the girls' knitting needles broke the silence under the lamp-light and the glow from the embers of the turf fire.

He began to tell a tale called 'Old Lord Erin's Son'. Throughout the tale he smiled or frowned at appropriate junctures, made comments like: 'Wasn't that smart of him?' and so on, while his family interpolated comments of their own: 'See that now' and 'Mark you'. I wrote from his transcription.

His power of vivid characterisation was astounding; his swift descents to whisper or hoarse croak just incredible. Unlike some traditional storytellers who religiously repeat and tediously recapitulate details of events occurring to a character, McAleer had an artistic sense of narrative talent which condensed with skill in proper proportion to the tale. Like McCullagh he kept pulling at his cap until the peak lay over one ear. He gave a quick smile as interlude each time he erected himself from his leaning stance on the bed but it vanished as soon as he leaned back and went on with the tale. Above all he unashamedly believed in the tale while he was telling it, as any good storyteller in any medium must believe, and was totally without halt, hesitation or inhibition in earthy detail or language when and where it was required: all, of course, within the purely rural norm when no 'outsiders' are present.

When he finished the tale he swung up from the bed, fished out his pipe and not until it was lit did he ask me what I thought of the story: without waiting for my answer he gave fuller details of the biography of the original storyteller and the events and incidents in his life, all of which I was noting as fast as I could. Then he remembered another tale told by a dead storyteller named Bradley and at once went into that one.

We did not have tape-recorders at the time (although other collectors did have Ediphones) but I noted details, motifs and notable idiomatic phrases in tales I was unable to get down. He told about half-a-dozen that night and remarked that had he known they would have been of use to anyone like myself he might have remembered them all. And better. He still had more tales, but he would have to think. And he gave a glance towards his wife.

I learned much later that she had heard the tales told in her own townland before her marriage and was helping to remind him.

The man both excited and mesmerised me. I had never heard such a flow of fluent narration, such a contrast of story.

It was very quiet and very late when, after tea had been made, and we had sat and smoked and talked he saw me to the road outside his laneway. Far below in the night over Glenhull the light from our own oil-lamp shone in the window. Alice was waiting up, her first night alone in the glen.

There were to be many more.

13 The Delicate Tread of Sex

The folklore collector, like the journalist, makes use of the topical tag. A wedding or wake or a christening, any event or calamity could provide the opening for long and deep inquiry on all such events in the past, the beliefs, practices, customs associated with each and so on.

Some such event in the locality while I was collecting general tradition from Annie McCrae revealed the possibility of a body of tradition in Human Life on sex beliefs of all kinds. I knew I was still very much a stranger – intruder in this sense; all the tradition would centre around some Glenhull person dead or still living. Annie may have been in her eighties at the time, but I was still a strange man! Here was a chore for Alice to give a hand: we had often discussed the possibility of co-operation on such delicate topics and had formulated the plan of approach.

It required shrewdness, perfect timing, and a kind of astuteness actually close to the cynical. The people around Glenhull may have sounded somewhat more naive than their counterparts in South Armagh, but there were economic factors to account for the distinction: the South Armagh people had emigrated both to America and England; farms were much smaller, the men forced to become dealers and hawkers or pedlars known as 'Pahvees' (an idiom which our Travelling People in the *ceant* use when referring to a group of unidentified incoming itinerants). The Glenhull soul was sound, however, the heart warm and genuinely hospitable; but naive or not as alert as a startled cat to any hint of deception.

The approach had to be shaped according to the nature of the mind to be warmed before yielding of its wealth of folk-honey. Inquiry would have to be deferred to afford a time lapse to evade suspicions of pure gossip: this worried because one was in a race with Death every day of the week.

(Alice by then reminded me that I might be claimed by the Angel myself: the work had more than momentum for me: it had become obsession. Yet, I still wrote the occasional special freelance articles, radio talks and features and completed a play called *Dust Under Our Feet,* a study of the intelligent illegitimate set in rural South Armagh against the familiar rural forces – broke Canon Law in my association of character but didn't know it – and had the satisfaction of seeing the play produced under Harold Goldblatt in The Old Group in Belfast and later in The Arts in London. I was told I would likely be ex-communicated. Sean O'Sullivan wrote happily over another huge collection but warned me to 'watch the health and take some recreation.' Writing was the only recreation I knew.)

Glenhull I now saw as a green urn laden with the secrets, the mysteries and characters of the past; but an urn suspended over an abyss by tapes of old roads held in delicate, frail hands. Anything could cause them to snap; the urn would tip; unknown wealth would sink out of sight for ever. As well as my race with Death radio aerials began to stretch across old sunken thatched roofs: this new groove of modernity and its attendant cynicism would langle me.

I had gained old Annie's confidence sufficiently to receive the injunction that I 'was not to tell where or from who I heard this from – or I might leave the country.' This was familiar – but heartening: a new stage had been reached. But the inner layers of material could be socially explosive.

It is a valid gimmick to prime a storyteller – awaken his dormant clan-instinct if you like – by telling a tale oneself, thus attributing its origin to an area outside his own. In other sections and categories of lore I could thread South Armagh's last folk whispers into a pattern of conversational query and attribute the whole fabric – not necessarily in fabrication – to a known or invented person in South Armagh: nothing very astute about such a design; but unless one knows the idiomatic vernacular and exclamations and sardonic remarks to flavour such approach to authenticity it will not deceive or impress the rural mind anywhere.

This is what Alice knew as well as myself; and she picked up where I had left off with old Annie – some inhibitions chiselled away – and out of the query came an astounding corpus of belief, even practice, that dared not be breathed in rural Ireland even to-day. The defensive complex in things folk (people expect it to be ridiculed and invoke a tone of self-ridicule themselves to form a screen) sharpens the innate shrewdness: one could be disastrously precipitate: one should make the approach more casual, take more time. But even without the grand race with The Angel of Death we hadn't time. There were equivocal jokes told around firesides in our youth to young and old, but only the older ones understood and yowled at the sexual implications. We peddled these too and found their Tyrone counterparts.

One school-master near Glenhull told me there was little folklore left; and that anyhow the people would not tell me anything if they could remember. I have given the reason why he, in all charity, said so: he simply did not know himself. Glenhull was a folk world brought to life as *The Tain* had been reclaimed. It could die again if we made a mistake: perhaps for ever.

And yet though there were motor-cars and post office telephones, wheel-less slide-cars still operated on the hilltops. Social clubs were starting in parish halls, with table-tennis and jazz, though film shows were forbidden. On a stretch of hillside one could see a tableau of work-patterns – tractor, horse and plough, the digging with the spade. Francis McBride used his stilts to take near-cuts over the Owenkillew. Always the two symbolic strands, the Christian and the pre-Christian, so intimately intertwined like Celtic tracery that decay of one caused the other to sag without anything better than derision of the dying to take the place of the vacuum.

Our house had become a noted ceili house for talkers. My father came before Spring, eager to see the children. He had his quota of folklore and folk tales to add to those of the visitors, and his sea tales and experiences delighted them. He thought the Gortin Glens and the district reminded him of winters in youth in the Highlands of Scotland; and when snow came one morning he couldn't be held. His eyes filled as he took leave of the boys next morning and I saw him off to Slieve Gullion on the train at Omagh.

I went back to constant collecting. Alice had made friends with local women and they all gave us material.

14   Advent of Spring

In February Michael Morris' mother died suddenly in Carnanransy. She was eighty-six years and he was very attached to her. I went to the wake.

I had never met the woman but Michael had quoted her so often as source for his material that I felt as if I had known her all my life: every folklore collector becomes involved in the lives and decades not only of the living but of the people they quote as sources, hence the strain on the collector's mental stamina.

I went with Francis Henry McBride on a gusty night, very cold: 'Cold Carnan' as the local phrases had it about Carnanransy, through which an old coach road from Omagh to Belfast once passed. Well-spaced lights in a line in blackness to our left were no longer strange to me: I had been there 'to the head of the town', as they said of the townland, to meet an old man named Donnelly.

At the wake-house door Francis Henry paused, raised the latch, raised his cap, blessed himself and prayed in silence. I did likewise. Then we went inside. In South Armagh it was the custom to walk in at once, raise the cap on entering and murmur: 'Lord have mercy on the dead.' We sat on a settlebed.

The corpse was laid out on the 'Cooltyee Bed' with the familiar surround of immaculate sheets and lighted candles within the bed and out of our sight. Women and girls sat on a long stool by the bed, the men elsewhere. Women who came in knelt in prayer at the bedside and then joined the company in talk of the dead woman and then on to mundane everyday topics. The men did not kneel in prayer.

A plate was passed round containing cigarettes and ready-rubbed plug tobacco. (Since the war no clay pipes had been distributed at wakes, although a local pipe-maker once lived and worked in the neighbouring townland of Broughderg.) I was eventually asked how we kept wakes in our country and I could truthfully reply: Much as you do here. Wake games had died out: although in South Armagh I had taken part in such boisterous wake-games as 'Marrying Out', a fertility ritual and purely pagan. Nothing like this had lived on in Glenhull in Tyrone, but very old men had heard older men talk of such games.

With Francis Henry I left the wake about midnight.

I cycled to look for new people in the daytime, wrote in the evenings, met those near at hand at night. The volumes began to mount up. Winter's claws in the remains of snow drifts on the hills were diminishing and slipping. I looked forward eagerly to spring. There had been days when rain, snow or sleet kept us housebound and dismal, irritable and depressed. Alice didn't comment on the implications of that row of telegraph poles rising up out and over the hill; her glance told me enough.

Francis Daniel McAleer had a wealth of material in tale especially; I spent as much time with him as I could. I was on my way to him one evening in early March when it seemed spring had been born in Glenhull: for half-an-hour I stood and let imagination run, forgot the storyteller and the expectations of the night at his fireside. I had walked the long hill from Glenhull to The Nine Pipes. Twilight was deepening. I stood and filled a pipe, looked back and down at Glenhull and our window light.

Into my mind came flecks of the folklore I had been gathering, especially about 'The Handy Women' who acted as midwives. A roofless house stood beside me, but outside lay rolls of earthy scragh. Someone was planning in hope for a re-roofing of new thatch, new promise, new hope.

I got the feeling that everything had somehow changed without the sound of a single breath or movement; the sensation quickened the blood. From the hollow came the sound of wild fowl: above me the whir of wings. Somewhere, faintly, a throat was cleared; a door slammed; I heard the tinkling of a burn like young hurrying feet. Mystery was afoot.

I knew that the lore I had collected was individualising the place, banishing the sense of initial hostility, filling everywhere and everything casual with personality: up there beyond the ruin stood another I couldn't see where Netchy, Francis Daniel's story source, had lived and died. I felt I knew the man. There was 'The Divil's Bush', a hawthorn, from which a limb had been cut to make a stake for a cow in a byre; with frightening supernatural results that very same night. Every outlined crest of hill, boulder, bush, house and bend of road were familiar and friendly to me in their lore and tradition. They lived. The very lights in the houses no longer stared; they now peered, knowingly. I could now name every one, saw behind each the welcoming wide hearths, the half-circle of ceilidhers breaking to make place for me in the vacated 'Chair of Pleasure'.

Even in the twilight I could discern the heights and hollows in their silhouettes: The Hill of Meen gently domed; Thornug in Crock with its Mass Rock. The names of Townlands danced in memory to their own word-music: Carnanransy where the jabbing headlights of a car bridged the Owenkillew to Formil; Altacamcosy and Curraghinalt, Coneyglen and beyond it Glenlark where one storyteller still survived.

Flecks of wool hung like mist on barbed wire along the road. Out in the darkness men were watching. I recalled that an early flock of Glenelly sheep had returned past our house from local winter grazing. The men, I was told, would head for Barnes or 'over the cut sod' – the turf-banks – to Glenelly, certainly one of the longest and most dramatic glens in Ireland. Rucked and rippling the sheep flowed the way a breeze was mucking a pool in the river, flowed over a low ditch like quicksilver till the dog bounded after them, swinging them this way and that and back on to the road: like wild-geese in flight.

'The bushes are chippin,' Francis McBride had said hopefully.

'The blackbirds are back on the street,' old Annie countered, seeing in this an omen of yet 'another layer' – of snow. Old Annie had added: 'But listen to the children though.' They had been making merry out of doors. The first ploughman was writing his score of promise in a scroll on a field hung on the side of Muninameal.

I remembered it all in the spring darkness gathering around The Nine Pipes and myself. I used to see Spring as a pageant prepared in the meaningless chaos of rehearsal, the idle chit-chat dialogue of unrelated talk, the bits and pieces of prop: all would eventually fit and blend and take one's breath away.

But I saw this Glenhull spring as an old cloaked woman bent in a hurry on a night of secret purpose, like The Handy Women of tradition. Her chortling was in the burn; her knowledge remote but potent like the glows from abandoned lights on the hilltops, with window-lights for brooches pinning her cloak about her. Her tread was in the memory of the beat of a single flail where Peter Keenan of Allwollies below had just that very day thrashed straw for thatch.

It was dark now. I walked on through Muninameal to the low, thatched house of my storyteller, still remembering the image of the old woman in her cloak bent on a night of mystery. Then a lamb bleated somewhere. Instantly I was reminded of my grandmother calling through the room door in Balnamatha at Slieve Gullion to waken us from the sleep of children:

'Rise with yous . . . Rise! Mornin's on the wall.'

'Rise with yous . . . Rise,' cried the woman in the cloak. 'Spring is on the glen. Rise!'

15   The Stations

I had collected much lore and tradition about the religious custom of 'The Stations', of which but the faintest memory survived at Slieve Gullion, but never actually took part myself until March.

'The Stations' were being held in the house of Pat McKenna of Carnanransy. Francis McBride had let me know the night before that he was going, and I knew he was a disappointed man; he had expected that the rota should have selected his own house, hence the renovation. When he called next morning about 9.00 I was taking a hurried breakfast; I wondered why his manner seemed restrained and put it down to the disappointment. (Until the announcement is made at Mass in church no one knows which house in a unit of three townlands has been selected. The custom dates from post-Penal days before Roman Catholics were allowed or capable of providing a church of their own.)

But McBride was downcast for a different reason. He said quietly, reprovingly:

'You're not fasting . . . ?'

I asked was it necessary for everyone attending to receive Communion and he said not, adding: 'I should have told you last night.'

For my part I was simply eager to observe.

We left on bicycles. A heavy fog filled the glen. There wasn't a sound or stir. On our way we overtook two black-shawled women near the crooked bridge of Carnan in the swooping dip of a hollow. Other people emerged out of the fog as we overtook them like figures appearing on a film negative under the developer. Some men were clad in their Sunday best, some wore only the 'Sunday coat' or jacket of navy blue serge over working overalls. We overtook more women, mostly wearing black shawls, a few in hats and coats: young girls wore contemporary attire, one being made-up like an actress on a set.

At the lane to the house we left our bicycles and slowly, solemnly walked up. I stayed two paces behind McBride, intent on watching him and the pattern of behaviour demanded by custom. The fog got thicker. We joined a group of men standing in the open door of a wide cart-house, which housed an iron-bodied lorry such as had brought me to Glenhull. Brief, hushed words of greeting were exchanged, a nod to me, then silence.

I knew some of the men by sight. More women arrived, walking in slow, processional gait; they went into the kitchen of the house while their men folk joined our group. Another silence. Then McBride said:

'I think we'll go a bit further.'

Joined by men from the group he went towards the house. I stayed where I was; I assumed rightly they were going to await and prepare for Confession. Gradually the men began to talk. I tried to look casual, knowing I was conspicuous and wishing I had stayed at home. More people ambled out of the fog and went towards the dwelling-house.

The men talked of a local man who had 'gone on the reel' in a drunken spree for some days around the public-house. One said:

'. . . Comin' up now I seen him put his head round McCrae's an' he'd scare his own mother. All dried blood and beard and dirt.' They laughed, then fell silent again till an aged tall man who was a bit stooped wearing a fine blue suit and brown hat came towards us. The quiet became distinctly deferential. I rightly surmised he was the man of the house. He said at once:

'Why don't yous come up the barn? It's warmer than here, men.' He hadn't noticed me at all.

No one answered, but they shifted on their feet. The fog was now black and bitterly cold. The old man didn't urge or coax the men but took out his pipe and stood with us, smoking in silence and like the others looked out at the fog. Eventually he made a joke about spring work and no sleep and someone said:

'You'll live a while yet, Pat.'

Someone said it was time the priest was arriving; and every time they heard a car thought it 'was his Reverence' but it was other old men, like Francis Frank Jack in his best clothes who had been given a lift. It was the custom, unless the household where 'The Stations' were being held had a car of their own, to hire one to bring the priest. They discussed this point, some disapproving.

A young man, hatless, appeared from the house, old Pat's son I presumed. He seemed to be checking or counting us. Old Francis Frank Jack called to him:

'You can take all these fellows in after an' give them their tea. There's not too many.'

Amid laughter the young man countered:

'I would only there's fast on. It just happens to be a contrary time, Francis.'

'Well', bantered Francis, pausing to let the laughter subside, 'a bottle of stout then, or a glass of whiskey. Try them with each.'

The priest arrived and went into the dwelling-house. Later, a girl appeared and stilled their laughter, spoke quickly to the young man and her eyes flicked over the men and rested on me. The young man hurried off: the priest had forgotten the Mass Book. The girl still stared at me. Suddenly I realised why and shook my head: she was counting the number due to receive Communion, a chore deputed to the family by the priest.

The men talked of preparations for turf-cutting, asked about help. James Porter, the miller of Glenhull, joined them, followed from the dwelling-house by another man who stood for a moment and quietly announced:

'He has all heard upstairs.' As if by concert, like a flock of startled snow-birds, everyone turned and hurried from the shed. I was left alone.

I looked at the fog; very embarrassed now; and had another impulse to go home. My absence would, however, make matters worse. I mused on the custom and what I had heard about it. And while I was doing so two men strolled out of the fog from the house and into the shed, looked at me reproachfully, nodded but said nothing. Each turned and looked out in silence at the fog. Almost unnoticed they turned and drifted from my side, walking between the lorry and the wall. I thought they had gone (as we used to say euphemistically in female company at Slieve Gullion for urination) 'to shed a tear for their country.' When they seemed to be overlong in rejoining me I looked around.

They were on their knees on the bare earthen floor.

The blood came to my head. They knelt with their backs to me, about a yard apart. They had removed their caps. I saw one man, then the other, turn his head slightly, knew they could see me. The only condoning gesture I could think of to proclaim my own instinctive sympathy and understanding, and to ease possible embarrassment, was to take off my own cap, which I did. One man then took out his Rosary. After about ten minutes they got to their feet, put on their caps, and rejoined me, without speaking, looking out again at the fog. Other men came from the house, paused in silence, then moved up the shed to kneel and pray.

In hushed voices they discussed the fog, its portents, the weather prospects, would it take a wind to shift it. Old Francis Frank Jack went by to kneel and pray, although I heard him remark that it was a bad place to kneel.

Next a shawled woman came to the shed, nodding without speech; the men stood aside to let her through. She held her Rosary in hands which clasped her shawl across her body. She knelt directly behind us at our heels. She was the only woman who came to the shed to kneel and pray.

When she left the men began to chat. Another recount was taken. Again I shook my head: perhaps it was all due to me anyway. Out of the fog someone called: 'No more to be heard?' Then a bell tinkled. As before the men moved up in a flock towards the house. I kept as close as I could to McBride but men crushed us apart going through the door.

Inside, every man removed his hat or cap and remained standing; but manoeuvred into groups so that a clearway was left in the centre of the floor with a passage to a room. The kitchen was fresh and spotlessly clean. A girl stood in attendance near a large modern range. An older woman sat looking after a baby in a handsome pram.

Quietly I moved and shuffled until I was at the back of the throng and picked a spot for myself close to a room door. I could have elbow rests on a chair at one side, a stool on the other. In younger days at the back of the chapel in Dromintee I had done my share of one-knee praying on the outside of one's 'good cap' or on a handkerchief – until sometimes the priest halted Mass and hooshed us up the church . . . Unless some of us bolted outside. We were apparently all very shy of being conspicuous. But I could no longer kneel without paralysing pain unless I managed to take the weight on my elbows. Someone maybe observed this, for one man motioned me to sit on the chair. Just then the priest began the Latin of the Mass in another room and everyone knelt on the kitchen floor.

The Mass went on. A second priest had already left in the hired car to attend the old and sick in the three townlands. They were expecting him, and I knew from collected tradition that, like Annie McCrae, those who could do so would be on their knees over a chair on the hearthstone, anticipating the time that this Mass was due to begin. At the Communion the priest moved among the people, carrying the chalice and white cloth which he handed to the first communicant, who held it under his chin while receiving The Host and then passed it on to the next. At last all had received and the priest remarked:

'That is all? Only two?' So I was not one lone bird after all.

The priest returned to the room and finished the Mass. When it was over everyone stood up. The front door had been closed during the Mass and was now swung open. A few shawled women left. An under-current of chat began. Only once did the baby in the pram whimper, and old Pat came up and began to fuss over it. Everyone except he had now replaced hats and caps on their heads. I kept my own in my hand.

On the kitchen table stood a brand new bucket. This contained Holy Water blessed by the priest and women produced or retrieved bottles, dipped them into the bucket, and went away, no-one corking a bottle. The girl of the house then appeared with mugs of tea but all the men politely declined, including myself. Now the priest divested, and in black soutane came from the room and sat at a table to begin collecting the stipends. Each man paid five shillings.

The fog was still thick as we left for home. On our cycles McBride remarked:

'It was a fair big Stations.'

He talked of old-time Stations. A dinner used to be supplied to the priest, but food rationing during and after the war discontinued the practice. He could recall priests who liked particular dishes and would remind parishioners of his palate when making the announcement in the Church. Whiskey also had to be provided. And as ever he could recall some anecdote.

Priests used go out fowling before a 'Stations' and one local man, suspecting that a neighbour had stolen his sheep, slipped into the room and invested himself in the soutane, stole and biretta from the chair on which the priest sat sideways while hearing Confession, with the curtains drawn on the windows. He called out: 'Anyone up there for Confession?' Confused, believing the priest to be on the moors, the suspected thief went to the room and with downcast head 'threw himself on his knees at what he thought was the priest's feet.' He confessed. The 'priest' took him over each Commandment; lingering long over: 'Thou shalt not steal.' The penitent denied he had ever stolen anything in his life.

The man impersonating the priest, pretending he had played a good joke, revealed his prank and confessed it himself to a priest who 'went wild with anger'.

'He had to go three times runnin' (consecutive weeks: as a penance) to The Island (Lough Derg Pilgrimage) for that. They said if he hada let on to give Absolution he would have had to go to Rome to The Pope.'

But McBride gave a guffaw at the tail-piece and hurried up his own lane, adding over his shoulder:

'You'll be thinking we're an awful wild people around here . . . '

He was gone before I could cap his story with similar events enacted by 'wild' characters impersonating priests in South Armagh. After all I had done so once myself – But only to 'scatter' a dance for fun. . .

16 Glenlark

Peter Pat Roe lived at the head of Glenlark, was old, had Irish and was said to have a wealth of tale and tradition. But the mouth of the glen never seemed to be free from its cover-curtain of rain, sleet or snow shower. And the last snow of spring fell when I first went in.

Not only is Glenlark the wildest glen I've ever been in it's the only glen with a stunning sense of loneliness all its own. All the misery and tragedy of remote rural Ireland seemed to have gathered in collective spirit in the place: you actually could feel life petering out before your eyes.

A road like an old hat-band sliding up the crown encircled the glen, one low down, the other from Gorticashel climbing the hillside. Blobs of 'waste' or ruined houses bloated the web of stone ditches. A few thatched houses survived. A loud river poured through a rocky course, emphasising the sense of desperate fleeing life, though every rock and waterfall had its folk story – with few to relate them. A strange insidious loneliness: the sort of place which roused a crazy urge to flee to the heart of a rowdy city amid people and the clamour of traffic.

Peter Pat Roe epitomised the tragedy and isolation of the place.

On my way up the narrow road I pushed through grazing cattle, one a young bull which glowered sullenly. The roof of a thatched house lay below the road; I could see down the chimney. A huge wreck of a house I took to be Peter's, but eventually a middle-aged man appeared from somewhere wearing an old RUC police uniform and a beret faded into a mixture of colours like petrol on a wet road.

He told me Peter lived in the next house and added without emotion: 'It's a house as bad-looking as this one . . . '

On the hillside the fading snow traced out the pattern of old abandoned corn or potato ridges here and there. The head of the glen itself simply ran out into the mountain which divided the place from Glenelly: somewhere here were noted boulders on an old Casan na Gorp, or The Corpse Road, along which funerals from Glenhull used to go, men carrying the corpse in relays, resting at the selected boulders, but never touching one drop of poteen until from the final boulder on the mountain-top the cortege was in view of Badoney below in Glenelly. Then came the drinking, the fighting, the ritualistic drawing of blood. Peter Pat Roe was said to know the route and the marking stones.

The cold was intense: winter had resharpened its claws of snow and was holding on. Then it began to rain out of a leaden sky. And then I was at Peter's house, the last residence next to the immense heath of the mountain.

There were a few bare trees around the house sieving a rising breeze with a sound which mimicked the waterfalls in the river. It was a two-storeyed house with holes in the slated roof. The gate hung awry on a lopsided pier. A famished flock of a mixed breed of fowl clustered around the threshold. The door was closed. There was no smoke from the chimney. Two calves as sullen with the cold as the young bull down the road stood dismally near the dung-hill. A fresh gust spilled through the trees like a breath of distant Spring trying to break the grip of winter so obvious all around me.

I knocked at the door. Inside a dog yelped. I waited. Knocked again and tried the latch. The dog barked and this time was chastised by a voice. After a long pause the door opened and a man stood before me, the half-door still between us.

He was tall, lean, with friendly grey eyes and he wore a heavy moustache. Despite the light in the eyes he looked dubious and suspicious. As well as an old British Army battle-dress tunic he wore a rough sack around his shoulders fastened on his chest with rough grass rope.

I told him who I was, where I was living, where I had come from, but not why I had called. All the time he looked at me he puffed his cheeks in and out, like a bellows. Without a word he turned from the door and went back up the kitchen. I followed.

Peter, a bachelor, lived alone. The kitchen was as gloomy as a closed forge and smelled worse. It was taken up with a bed fronted by a dresser laden with old delph, and from which on hooks hung an assortment of garments — several caps like the one he was wearing, towels, shirts and sundry cloths. There was no fire in the open grate: a young black and white dog lay in fact curled up in the ash where the fire should have been burning.

Peter, still without a word, sat on a stool at the fireside facing the front window. I sat on a backless chair beside the table, which was stained with the leakings as of thatch: suddenly I remembered that the house was slated. Casually and unobtrusively I looked up to the ceiling.

Through holes in the ceiling I could see other holes in the room and the roof above filled with the thickening grey sky of storm.

Beside him (hanging from a curved support bar of the fire-crane), was the only night illumination: a tilly lamp: a simple tin affair of a container with a thin spout or 'stroop' like an oil-can and a bit of rag drawn through for a wick.

Eventually he asked me who and what I was and I told him. Again he lapsed into silence, except when he stamped his feet on the flagstones in the cold. He was suspicious of me and my trade and I knew it although I knew that Gaelic enthusiasts and musicians – for he played the flute or fiddle – called with him now and then to extend the vocabulary. But he knew these people or knew of them.

In the end I got him talking although his taciturn lapses irritated and exhausted me. I was told the route of the old funerals, tales and traditions: his father had been on such funerals. It was fiendishly cold, the dog still curled up in the grate. Not once did Peter refer to the absence of fire – no doubt his own turf lay wet out on the mountain. Under a table he had piled a few split boards and bundles of raw-shoots from a hedge.

I stayed with the man until finally the weather chased me. Sleet fell and turned to rain. When it began to seep through roof and ceiling it gathered in a dank pool on the table; then began to stain my raincoat like coffee, spatter the note-book, although I kept discreetly moving my chair to evade or to 'jook the drops', moving and moving again.

All the dank odours of the house impregnated my clothes. Peter's dispirited mood and suspicious personality – the spate of sudden talk like Glenlark river – the following dead silence as in a wake on a young death – all clung to my own mind, body and spirit. The legacy was a terrible headache.

He could be genial but his taciturn breaks and the sense of death crouching in the glen affected me like a weird pageant of the macabre. Peter seemed to act as if he knew he was playing a central part – unwillingly and in silence – but compelled to carry on . . . To hang on as jovially as he could.

Nowhere have I found a man and a glen with matching, inter-changing personality such as I found in Peter Pat Roe in Glenlark.

17 Man With a Sense of Humour

I have yet to meet a man with such a rich sense of humour as Francis McBride: it could be impulsive, spontaneous, mischievous, verbal or an act in silence that took intelligent planning. And yet he was a busy man, never idle on his farm, but never failing to call in to relate a fleck of lore which set off some lengthy inquiry; or to name a possible narrator he had remembered; or to arrange for a bicycle trip to visit a man he knew, usually with Michael Morris along, even as far as Glenelly beyond Barnes, where the Sperrin range made a sublime backcloth.

We had become integrated now. He knew we liked fish, especially herring and we missed this on the diet: only the old style board-hard ling or the barrel of salted herring were to be had. He remarked that if in Cookstown he would see what he could do.

One day a pony-drawn spring van came trotting the road and a voice gave the loud chant of:

'Herrin'-loy – Her-loy – Her-loy – Her-loy.'

I was typing in the room, Alice busy in the kitchen. Both of us yelled about grabbing a plate and getting out to stop the fellow before he drove past. We both charged out hollering.

Out of the back of a strange van clambered a man. It was of course McBride who, when the van-man called with him on other business and was going home to Gortin, was unable to repress his impish sense of humour. I felt so stupid – Salt-water herrings from Lough Neagh!

There is probably more wit than humour in the North of Ireland – unfortunately: religio-political tensions have sharpened one at the expense of the other; even good-natured social banter between the opposing religious blocks (and there is social contact in places like Glenhull) demands that each maintain the prestige of its own side: again simply another aspect of a traditional uppermanship exemplified in the Irish custom at wakes of repartee contests between representatives of townlands of districts: 'Camping' and 'Throwing Mobs' are idioms for this practice.

But wit must leap as if ignited by the end-word of the phrase which fires it: humour must have time to dander. The folklore collector also has to inquire into wit and humour and its protagonists and leave speculation and analysis to others.

With McBride it was – as wit is – a gift. He could no more suppress this tendency than a bird can resist flying, or a trout swimming. He would sometimes escort me to the house of a new narrator and begin:

'Peter? This is the new pension officer who wanted to know where you lived.' Apprehension would widen the old man's eyes and stay with him sometimes all through the evening. Or was I 'a new man taking the tillage?' Or checking up on Government subsidies on land? When Proinsias O'Conluain of Radio Eireann came to Glenhull to record the surviving native speakers a huge van then had to be used for disk-recording with long cables and all the rest, the driver-cum-engineer Dermott Maguire working outside. The van of course bore a crest and created curiosity and talk.

To some very old people McBride had his own explanation:

'It's a man sent in that yoke from The Pope in Rome to see that yous all make the jubilee.'

Some of his own earlier pranks have gone into folk tradition. Several times he had scared people with impersonation of 'Mock ghosts'. In one he had to call upon a confederate. With another neighbour they were card-playing one winter. The prank demanded a bright moonlight night. Through a high-banked road around the cut-away bog leading to the card-house several low tunnels had been cut to provide passage for flood water. In these McBride hid two white sheets. On the moonlight night he made an excuse from the card-playing and went outside. His confederate later did likewise. The neighbour, an addict for 'The Divil's Prayer-Book' as the cards were called in tradition (and there were tales a-plenty on the subject in Glenhull) finally realised that neither had returned and he would have to return home alone: when card-players according to tradition might meet any and anything 'not of this world'. He set off at once.

He began to whistle to 'keep himself company'. Then a white-shrouded object darted from behind a clump of heather on a turf-bank stub, shot into the roadside and disappeared. His whistling stopped, he blessed himself, murmured a prayer, tossed his pack of cards out of his pocket – and ran. A hundred yards or less further on the white object – the second conspirator – shot out from the road bank and disappeared into the heather.

'God a-Christ – Before me already.'

He didn't collapse but charged back to the card-house, had to be escorted home and lay in bed for a week. McBride, upset and alarmed at the unexpected outcome of a sick man he had simply hoped to frighten for a joke explained the trick. The man of course refused to believe him. But he never played cards again.

In another prank McBride exemplified exquisitely the difference in mood and temperament between wit, which can never really be called kind, and humour, which can.

A flood washed away the old bridge over the Owenkillew between Teebane and Aghasruba, where McBride had been born, and the authorities decided to abandon the old and replace it with a new bridge, built with concrete pillars and supports, then a new idea in bridge construction. Until living memory people had used fords at these spots, and McBride retained his stilts of course. Concrete was not new but was modern in Glenhull, where such articles as flails for threshing existed alongside threshing-mills drawn by steam traction-engines, later displaced by the tractor.

McBride asked the engineer in charge when the new bridge would be open as his own thresher was isolated in Aghascruba and he was anxious to resume work. The date was more than two weeks ahead. The manual labour was local. So the work was rushed and the heads of the contracting firm from Derry came to watch McBride drive his thresher over the new bridge; the workers were far from pleasant when they realised the cause of the rushed work exerted from them.

Of course McBride calmly walked back over the new bridge with an old flail under his arm.

Another day he scared the living daylights out of a turbaned Indian pedlar for no other reason again than an irrepressible sense of impish fun. Preparing for 'The Stations' he was mixing red distemper in the barn when the Indian called and went into the kitchen where McBride's wife, Sarah, kept telling him she wanted none of his wearables: like the Travelling People some of the Indians by dress and manner imposed on people and compelled them to buy because of fear.

McBride was wearing old clothes in readiness for the job of distempering a room. He stripped to his old shirt, stained it with the distemper, picked up an old butcher's knife and sharpening stone, stained both and went into the kitchen. He spoke to no one but, pulling a face, stood sharpening the knife – which appeared to drip blood – and paused only to glare at the Indian, who fled, abandoning his pack open on the floor. The joke came back on McBride as he had some difficulty in the following weeks ascertaining who the owner was, then living in Derry, so that the pack could be returned to him.

18 'Ploughin' The Headrig Anymore'

It had better be stated that no narrator was paid or expected payment for the folklore they gave. On the contrary they seemed to think they owed me an obligation because I had bothered to listen and write tradition down from their lips. With the aid of my neighbour-narrators I had now a wide circle, supplemented with discoveries of my own: yet men called from distant townlands and told me of people who would be glad to tell me anything they knew if I thought it of value.

This was touching. There was an old man named Donnelly who lived at 'the head of the town' that is, townland. I had been with him several times; he was frail, though still tall, but gaunt. I was always concerned lest I over-tax the strength of such people and would deliberately avoid calling. I heard one day John Donnelly had been ill and called out of pure social honour and because I liked the man.

He welcomed me in the traditional way, looked weaker, his grip without power. But he joked:

'I could have been puttin' in my Purgatory under a bush since I seen you last.' (It is part of the lore of The Lone Bush that the souls of the dead, as well as the fairies, spend part of their Purgatory under local Lone Thorns.)

I chatted, then rose to go. He seemed disappointed: because I had not got on to folklore. He began to tell a long piece of narration and was clearly tiring himself. I tried to stop him, said I would call again when he was better. He said:

'Sit and ask me whatever you want. I don't want to take anything of value to you or to anyone coming after away with me. Sit and ask me your fill: for I'm ploughing the head-rig anymore.'

The head-rig of a field is the last to be ploughed: he was likening the life-span to a field. He knew his own was shortly to be finished. I sat and listened and wrote.

He was not the only one who had said something like that: was not to be the last.

Instinctively the people, though yielding to shoddy modern ridicule, ill-informed if not blatantly ignorant, pretended to laugh off their knowledge of tradition while secretly respecting it: innately feeling its worth and heritage which haunted a man like his own shadow. People certainly knew some traditions were good, some bad; some could be re-shaped, some should be discarded. But no tradition can be re-shaped until events and life and a revolutionary force demands the change with the thrust of a people behind it: just as no custom or tradition can be honestly revived to preserve a sentimental comfort in illusion: what a people require they will take: what they discard they dismiss for good.

Francis Daniel the able storyteller of Muninameal overlooking Glenhull, continued to remember and recite his 'old rehearsals' as well as general lore. If I failed to call he would wonder why and look offended. Again I did not want to presume too much on him or anyone.

But one night when I called without warning he seemed dejected and remarked off-hand that he doubted if he could recall any more tradition. I did not press: he had already filled more than a volume of tales alone.

We chatted and smoked and I left early. Spring had come and people were trying hard to catch up on work in the land held up by bad weather. Lights in the houses went out earlier than usual and we had no visitors.

One morning I was writing in the room where the window gave me a view of the far glenside of Muninameal in good sunlight. Everyone was busy in the land. I could see Francis Daniel in shirt sleeves working with a graip or four-pronged fork at weeds in one of his own fields.

The Glen to our disappointment, depressing on dull days, refused to blush green on the hilltops but held on doggedly to its brown of peat.

I watched Francis. Every now and then he stopped and leaned on his graip. I wondered why he was so worried. His wife I heard had not been so well lately. I was nevertheless concerned lest in some unwitting way I had offended him, because like McCullagh he could be touchy, especially if suspecting a slight.

(When McCullagh's folk knowledge and his craft became known he was taken by newsmen into Omagh to be photographed. Somehow he suspected a slight and, as one journalist afterwards told me, left them in a daze as if a hurricane had whirled in and out. Few appeared to understand the nature of the dignity such men cherished.)

I forgot Francis Daniel and went on with my work and was still absorbed when he tore up to our gate on his bicycle, still in shirt sleeves. His face was alight. He came in crying for me to 'bring the printer' (my typewriter) to the kitchen as he had a tale to tell. (I had typed some of his material straight from his narration.) He began to explain. For over a week he had been trying to recall parts of a tale which eluded him: explained he had been doing so the night I called to find him morose: he had been upset because 'it wouldn't come, not all the parts.' All had come back to him while working in the field: he had abandoned everything and rode like blazes to me. I must take it down while it was clear in his mind. In turn I was upset because his enthusiasm was taking him from his work and said so. He waved his arms to dismiss my concern. Get the tale down at once – he'd be more worried if it slipped his mind again. It was one he had heard partly in Gaelic and the translation in English he had heard was hazy.

He sat on a chair with his back to the front window while I sat beside him with the typewriter before me. He talked: I typed like hell. Alice made tea. He waved it away and talked – living as usual through its moods, characterising its people, making the complimentary or derogatory comments as interludes for breath pauses, growing stern-faced, eager, anticipatory, sullen or gay as events in the tale-telling demanded.

When he had finished he said nothing but took up the tea, now cold, refused to wait until a fresh pot would be made, got to his feet, looked through the window at the 'country mad working' and remarked on the fine day it was, thank God: just as if he were someone who had dropped in to light his pipe from the fire: as if totally unaware of what he had just achieved and demonstrated.

And then he was off.

I had suggested, in lieu of tea, a call to Jimmy McCrae's pub. He declined: he was a man who could take a drink or leave it alone; and, anyhow, he said the McCrae boys would be in the land working. He had to get back at once to his own.

I went in to look over my hurried typing of his tale. Looking up later I saw him back in the field working without pause.

Like a log which dams a stream the tale he couldn't remember released a flood of others in the weeks ahead. Then came an estrangement. He was a keen Crosswords fan and thought I should be able to help, in fact insisted. I hesitated, fearing that my own interpretation of clues were going to be incorrect without a doubt, while his own stood a better chance. He seemed to think I didn't want to help, failed to call with me, and was not in his house when I called. I wanted to show my gratefulness to the man in some positive way. In the end when we met he said he had no more stories, dismissed my praise of his gifts and in folk-storytelling, guffawed over the the contretemps of the Crosswords, but I wasn't convinced. He had imagination but it never seemed to be able to function except when he told a folk-tale.

I had to accept that he was finished with tale-telling, no longer respected me, and would relapse into the odd-looking man he had been when I had first met him – how many months, years – decades since I had come to Glenhull?

One becomes involved in so many aspects of the generations that the impression of prolonged, ubiquitous life is no illusion: one knows everyone's story in more depth and detail than any neighbour could possibly be aware of: one is told information close to the heart that no confessor would ever hear.

Right or wrong in such reflection I was wrong about Francis Daniel. He was even more interested in the folk-tale than I was myself and would prove his enthusiasm in the days ahead.

19 Interlude In Lore-Hunting

I had drained part of the swamp behind the house to make ridges for vegetables. Rhubarb roots brought from Slieve Gullion were planted too. In a sack I hauled stones from the river bank and pitched the pathway round the house, dug up gravel and sloped it to run off winter rains. The inside walls had been white-washed. The place was habitable-looking anyway.

The smoke was a bother: although by then I had been in thatched houses where chimneys had been deliberately planned to cause the turf-smoke to curl out slowly into the upper part of a kitchen, so that the oil-lamp burned like the sun in an evening summer fog; when a tall man stood up to leave he spoke unseen, his head like a mountain immersed in the mist, as in Peter Rosie Keenan's of Alwollies near Glenhull: the house where two genial bachelor brothers gave tea in big blue-rimmed bowls, and where the 'pipe of hospitality', whatever about hygiene and concepts of contagion, was passed round from mouth to mouth during a night of talk and story-telling: a clay pipe that is: when pressed to accept I always claimed that a clay sickened me. Then I would be offered cigarettes.

Annie McCrae relied on me to bring some messages, and with her neighbour women brought Alice into their circle. Out of this came fine lore – as the Infidelity Test: the putting of a suspected woman, naked, into a shed with a bull; if the bull attacked it would prove her guilt. (A bull is supposed to be terrified of the human in the nude.) All told of course in relation to an actual event involving some local person.

The only blacksmith surviving in the area was Keenan the Smith in Altacamcosy, a complacent man who had tradition to relate, and with a hand-bell to display which he had accidentally found near a site in a local glen where Mass used to be celebrated in the Penal Days.

Patrick's Day we spent in McCrae's pub, where Jimmy (dark and tousled haired, he had spent some years in Australia) – parried the crowd. Someone called for a round including a lemonade.

'I sell no lemonade on Patrick's Day.

When whiskey was ordered:

'Is it singing whiskey, talking whiskey or fighting whiskey yous want?'

The pub was one of the oldest in the area, with low broad counter, a few shelves, a few bottles, the usual distiller's mirror with gold-crested adver-tisement, and little more. One long stool ran along the wall between the bar and the post office. From the post office a thumping sounded when closing time came.

Poteen could no longer be procured in the parish since it was in the Diocese of Derry, in which the bishop had declared poteen-making to be a Reserved Sin. Some said it was 'no harm to make a drop', others claimed it had 'closed houses in the parish.' It was common for men to gather in a house after Mass with a poteen-maker: following the imposition of the episcopal decree from Derry he served liquid ether instead – in half egg-shellfuls.

There was a story of the last run of poteen made in the parish.

It concerned two Munterloney men who made a run of poteen after the decree had been issued. Then their consciences became troubled, urged by their women-folk. They honoured their bishop but were not prepared to face him in his seat in Derry City. The solution lay in the hope that at the next Stations old Father Peter McGeown – one of themselves – would stretch a point, hear their Confessions, and the thing would be forgotten. All in their townlands knew of their predicament and the proposed solution.

The day of The Stations the people assembled in the farm-house kitchen. The priest was in the room. By tacit consent the two poteen-makers were to be allowed go first. One man went, closing the door. He returned sooner than expected, met the questioning stare of his companion and announced:

'No good: the case is adjourned to Derry.'

The folk-mind then took over from folk-fact and told how the two men on appointment went to Derry. One remained in hiding on a cold March day while the other faced his bishop. He was a long time in coming out. He had received as penance and to make atonement for his sin: that under no circumstances or by any means or method was he to communicate with anyone until he had crossed his own threshold back in Glenhull in Munterloney.

So that when his confederate asked how he had got on he made dumb signs: at which the other exclaimed:

'Holy God if he struck you dumb I'm far enough.'

Not until they had reached home could his companion enlighten him.

A good tale to help drown The Shamrock on any Patrick's Day anywhere. And they swore every word was true.

20 The Last Druid in Ireland

One night Michael Morris brought to our house a young, heavily built man who wore heavy horn-rimmed glasses, quiet, and dark. His name was Larry Loughran, a native of the area, then teaching in Cookstown sixteen miles away. He had heard of me and my work and was interested in folklore; in fact in writing generally.

Of his integrity and gentle sincerity there was no doubt: I was certain I had met him somewhere before. (He had in fact been a model for a character in one of the Tyrone novelist Benedict Kiely's books.) Loughran knew of my short stories but not of me and was surprised, he said, to find I was the same man: he had expected a much older man. He surprised me by saying that Ben Kiely was an Omagh man, would soon be in his home town and that he would write and let him know.

I knew nothing of the Irish literary world or its figures except a few names, although I had contributed special articles and short stories to several papers and magazines as well as to radio. So when Benedict Kiely wrote that he could meet me in Omagh I rode in one day on the bicycle, aware from press notices that his second novel had just been published.

Kiely was a much younger man, boyish indeed, than I had expected. I liked him at once. His manner of swift change from serious demeanour to bursting smile at first puzzled me, especially some of the silences: I feared I was not only boring the man in my shyness but keeping him from a more congenial occupation. I did not then understand his magnificent range of mental versatility, his profound literary knowledge; he expected me to know something at least of people and books and trends he mentioned, when in fact I knew sweet damn all. When we got on to social issues in Ireland, particularly rural Ireland, I was on home ground; and walking around the streets of hilly Omagh, with its imposing Courthouse set in domination at the head of the hill – as landlord's houses and barracks were often set to dominate the people – he delighted me with the sane-minded sureness about the issues running the country to seed – and slow death.

I had written that it was the insidious slow trickle of emigrants that was the danger: if only a whole townland could be induced to rise like a flock of crows and squat on municipal or national legislative buildings the dramatic effect would either shock or scare the powers in control to apply remedies. Neither of us could foresee that within less than twenty years the Marchers and Sit-Down Squatters would be compelled to do just that for their own convictions.

He pointed out the settings of some of his stories and books. He liked my folk plays and my stories; he liked the work I was doing, but wondered why I wasn't writing more creative material as well. I lacked his facile pen and its consistent high merit; but he understood, with some awe, when I explained the range and extent of my folk collections in Glenhull alone. He heard how even a patch of old abandoned ridges under moss or heather showing like the ribs in a hound haunted me obsessively until I had tried to unearth its story and the people who made it.

He took me to meet his parents – his father, who had been a soldier, knew Glenhull. Later that evening he and his brother-in-law got two bicycles and, true to tradition, conveyed me a-wheel as people I visited walked 'The Three Steps of Courtesy' when I left. We rode beyond Mountfield, where the poet Alice Milligan used live, to Killyclogher. I knew of a few narrators in the district, a man with ballads and songs, Kiely sang folk songs as we rode along.

Far ahead the Sperrins cowered. My instinct anticipated rain, and much as I was enjoying this company and the spin I tried to persuade them to return. Neither wore coats. I prophesied a deluge.

When the rain began they said it would be a passing shower: to me it was to be, as we'd say in South Armagh 'long-tailed and heavy'. So it was. We sat first under a tree, I talking of folklore I had collected, making comments, relating it to the diminishing life of the countryside. The tree begin to drip and we took shelter in a wee house where we were welcomed by a small decent Orange-woman who wanted to make tea for us. With the rain easing off we left. Still they insisted on riding further; and all the time we talked, sheltering once more when the deluge resumed. Youngsters on bicycles in the spirit of youth that is indifferent to rain whooped and cavorted past us. More comment, though I forget what I said.

Long after with rain still falling we parted, they for Omagh, myself for the overcast country of Munterloney and Greencastle and Glenhull. They must have been sopping wet. Despite a mac the water ran from my boots when I got as far as Eddie MacCullagh's pub to shelter.

Kiely remembered it all and wrote:

'The tumult of the passing of the youngsters on their way to a Mission in the local church at Killyclogher aroused and inspired my companion and he began to speak. He treated me to a long monologue on Ireland, a long speech of wise words on the ground and history of Ireland, the ways of her people, the folk tradition, and in the end he came down to the destiny of our young people in the world we live in to-day.

'It was informative and moving and suddenly I thought: "This man here beside me is a Druid, as much a part of this ancient land as the stone he sits on. He could have been here on this hillside under this oak before Patrick came. For such close wisdom could only come from centuries of meditation . . . A Druid from the land around Fionn Mac Cumbaill's Mountain in South Armagh . . . " '

He has alluded to 'Druid' several times since: his words amazed me as much as that allusion to 'druid' amused. When his novel *The Captain of The Whiskers* reached me he inscribed it to 'The Last Druid in Ireland' and I enjoyed the joke.

That is why I have serious inquiries even to-day from the United States about my 'druidism' . . .

I really thought I had left all wisdom behind about the age of twenty-one: or when I had uprooted myself from Slieve Gullion itself. In truth I now felt that if I did not actually know Finn McCool he was an uncle, his adversary The Cailleach Bearea – witch or not – an aunt!

21 Cromwell and The Irish Dead

No collection went to the Folklore Commission in Dublin without a sound contribution taken down from Padraig McCullagh: all collected in our own house. I had tried to find him at home several times, night and day, and at last was successful, but only when I had chased around Aughinamerrigan hill back and forth on my bicycle: he was crossing to and from directly over the hill, had heard I was searching for him, and was on one side of the hill when I was on the other.

In late evening I found him at home in Curraghinalt, working in his forge. Keenan the Smith was his neighbour; but McCullagh did no work except for himself. I found him facing the coulter or cutting-knife of the horse-drawn plough.

McCullagh hardly bothered with persiflage or familiar chit-chat, but always launched right away into something traditional: anything and everything recalled some associated account of Community or Work Lore. He was not truly a folk-story teller, preferring the Historic and Local Event, but conscious of the pattern at old fireside ceilis would oblige and tell a tale as best he could; always first in Gaelic, then in his own translation; but as a reciter, not a story-teller such as Francis Daniel.

The floor of the shed where he did his forge work, with bellows, upraised hearth, tools and anvil was as rough as any mountainside. He limped badly as he moved to and fro, a man who was over-working himself in the land. He believed in the land. He believed in tradition, but never hesitated to criticise if he thought such out-moded. He was Republican by politics, but never intolerant. He had some tales of The Fianna, and would re-tell one about Cromwell because he believed it carried a lesson which he thought our people should take to heart.

His grandfather had told the tale, in Gaelic of course. Cromwell was on the march with his army in Ireland hastening to lay siege to another town and took a near-cut. On a narrow-passage they met with a funeral. Neither would make way for the other. Cromwell's commanders prepared for battle, the Irish to resist, but Cromwell intervened for a parley, stating that the battle would cause serious delay whatever the outcome.

So he approached the 'friends of the corpse' and offered to buy it from them. They were scandalised. He increased the amount of his offer and increased it again until it was so tempting the Irish sold the corpse, turned it over to Cromwell, stood aside and let him and his army pass, taking the corpse with them.

He said to his commanders:

'Let that be a lesson to yous: a people that would sell their dead will sell anything. You don't have to fight.'

In the forge he talked of other traditions. I watched him with astonishment: not once amid his work and handicapped-walking did he pause – all in his fast hearty husky voice, sometimes barely touched by a fleeting short laugh if the narration called for lightness. And all the time he was working on the coulter. Smiths of course used tongs to handle such a hefty hunk of iron when it came red hot from the fire: McCullagh used his own method. Snatching the cap from his head in the left hand he used it as hand-cloth on the coulter in the fire, whisked it over to the anvil and began to wield and batter it with a small sledge in the right hand. Several times the cap burst into flame; hardly interrupting his talk amid the ringing anvil he blew out the flame. When he had finished he chucked the cap back on to his head. It still smoked. He cooled the iron and then apologised for his hurry: he had an hour or two to do in the farm across the hill. But when the pressure of the work eased he would be up to see me.

But, like many other people I hardly knew he called back to me:
'You're not wantin' a bite to eat? A man on the road finds hunger.'
I said not.

'I'd be highly vexed,' he said, 'and so would Mary' – he meant his sister – 'to know you went past my house wantin' meat or drink, hungry or dry. It's the custom in this country an' always was to make a bite to eat for any traveller you welcome.'

Since our own house was one of the very few along the roadside we had had our share of callers, who, knowing the custom of hospitality, walked in, sat down and as we knew expected tea. It was not such a self-consciously respected custom at Slieve Gullion, but no one looked on a cup of tea and bread, or a share of what was eating, as making a meal.

So we had Tramp Blacksmiths who had been through the country years before: deaf and dumb mutes who had to be housed in the loft of the kiln of the mill, or tramp pedlars with a line of blarney selling items like combs, wooden clothes-pegs, studs, safety-pins and so on.

One of these, when Francis McBride was present, took his stock from the butt of a sopping wet sack – it was pouring when he called – and held up a marmalade-dish to Alice.

'Cheap', he said, 'and like myself: Orange.' He said he came from one of the 'blackest Prodesan spots in all Ireland, The Birches outside Portadown where you might have heerd the Pope has a helluva bad name.' He claimed to have been over forty years on the road since he left the British Army after the First World War. Jokingly McBride asked if he could get him a 'good tight woman round Portadown.'

Familiar with this line of banter I cut in: 'Scores. Best county in the Ireland for them.'

'Now you're talkin',' beamed the tramp. To McBride he said solemnly: 'But you have a lady.'

'How would you know?'

'The burnt smell is off you – Like this fella here.'

Another traditional line of course. The tramp added quickly: 'Mister – If me an' you got two stout young strappin' butts of women the sort you mention – at our time o' day there'd be nothin' left of either of us but the braces.'

I think this embarrassed Francis, but the tramp went on to talk of Folk Cures (of which I had been collecting a glossary), offered to tell of all and any cure, even for my thinning mop. He added: 'I knew a girl lost her hair out the Ballygawley road was cured and we can cure you. But it may turn badger grey. But it's a real old cure.'

'With goose-droppings, paraffin oil an' sheep's lard,' I said. 'Ground in the dust of the burnt jaw of a boot.'

'You take the words out of me mouth.'

I was quoting an Armagh folk-cure supposed to restore hair to the knees of a horse stripped in a fall in a bad gap! He didn't wait to make a sale, but whipped up all in his hand and went off, whistling merrily though the rain pelted.

He knew Porter the Miller and expected to stay there for the night. Alice cried that she wanted to buy his dish – and told me to make tea – but first get the fellow back. He was hatless and coatless but when I went out was nowhere in sight.

But another man was walking in the rain. I stood in the shelter of the turf shed till he came up.

He complained of the rain. The land would be lost. God was angry with the world and people. No sign of it taking up. A pity of the people.

He had been filling his pipe. He said absent-mindedly:

'I came to a loss myself this morning.'

The Owenkillew I knew was in flood. He said:

'My woman died just at 2.00 o'clock.'

A fair selection of comprehensive gossip of any place isn't a bad measure to use in a hurry to run up a graph of the social history, the attitude and temperament of a people. This, anyway, was folklore as valid as McCullagh's story of Cromwell and the Irish dead.

Just as another piece of gossip had to be noted when an accident outside the wee town of Gortin (where the denizens refer to its environs as 'out in the country') involved a loaded cattle-lorry, its driver and helper. The talk naturally had been of the injuries to the men. One man listening said nothing until he asked: 'Who did you hear owned the cattle?'

Or the man coming home in his laden cart and horse from Cookstown. Not having left with 'the curse of the town on him' and hurrying to get to a local auction he fell off near his home and a wheel passed over both legs, breaking them. Old women in panic carried him into a near-by house, laid him across the hearth-stone, unconscious. While some hurried for priest and doctor others doused the legs with hot water. He revived and even managed to rise on one elbow. They cried, keened and lamented. He cried louder at them to shut up. In the quiet he asked:

'That auction up the road the day? Who got the land can you tell me?'

And one wet Sunday on my way to Mass I got as far as The Nine Pipes when the deluge came in liquid rods. I sheltered in an out-house of the ruin where the scraghs were ready for re-roofing, finally in the rain rode back down the hill home again. The blinding rain made its own screen.

Later that afternoon Alice called on old Anne McCrae who as usual asked: 'Well? What news's?'

There was nothing to relate (we seldom had!) except to add that neither of us had got to Mass.

'Aye . . . ' says Annie, 'sure don't I know. When he got as far as The Nine Pipes he coulda got the rest.'

All good until integration brought it home as sharply as whin thorn and it got irritating: the price had to be paid.

22 People From Home

I was writing in the room one day when a figure hurried up the steep path to the door. As soon as I heard the inflection of the voice I knew it was South Armagh taking its time over the depths of vowel, not abbreviating a single syllable or letter, except of course any final 'g'.

At the door I recognised the man as quickly as he recognised me: a Pahvee from the village of Jonesboro. His name was Morgan.

No self-respecting Pahvee would agree to be called a Pedlar. He has sold cloth and suit-lengths from the Arctic at Dawson, through The Dust Bowl and every city, to Mexico, Australia with calls to New Zealand and Tasmania: one of them prized the piece of plaster he had gouged from the wall of Newryman and patriot John Mitchel's cottage out there. The home-runs were more a pastime.

He stared at me, then the smile broke slowly; he spat into the heart of his hand, I into mine and we shook. But he wouldn't come in: 'You know how it is, Mick. Up the road to make a shillin' or lose two. We would talk too much.' He told why he had called. People in some local house where he had called in hope of a sale (and he would have his story, lies or truth, right of course) observed that he spoke very like a man named Murphy in 'The Bungalow'. A man writing folklore. He knew I was interested in folklore, knew I wrote; but as he said himself:

'No Drementee man would be mad enough – folklore or not – to come an' live in such a wild lonely place.' He couldn't believe it could be me and had to see for himself

At Slieve Gullion I hadn't been missed!

'Ah well, no matter. Always a Drementee man no matter where you go. Heaven an' Hell I suppose it'll be the same.' And then naturally wanted to know if I could put him on to 'a few marks' – prospective customers. I pleaded the ignorance of the stranger. Pahvees only told lies where the truth didn't suit. As one of them said about his religious son whom he was neglecting to introduce to the graft:

'He'd be no good: he wouldn't tell a lie.'

I still kept my hand in with the occasional article, story or radio talk for the BBC: as far as I knew I would be jobless in less than eighteen months and relying again on my wits. One talk in Belfast took place Saturday evening and I got as far as Cookstown the following day around 5.00 in the evening. I was expecting a lift for the sixteen miles to Glenhull but my people wouldn't turn up until 7.00. And in the North on Sunday hardly a parachute would open, not in the towns anyway. I set out to walk. 'Long hungry Cookstown,' said the tramp, one hard frosty morning: 'Where every stone is tied and every dog is loose.' It has a handsome, wavy wide street a mile long, but however affable its citizens is a dreary place on any Sunday. I hadn't eaten since 1.00. I set off.

People knew I was a stranger and stared. They spoke when spoken to or gave a nod, otherwise passed on: those who replied knew 'which foot I dug with' – usually.

· Near Orritor (where I had taken down traditions of 'The Stranger's Fair' – Planter's that is) two vicious dogs attacked me. I walked in the hope of meeting possible narrators but ahead could see thunder clouds darken the sky to deep navy blue, and from a rise saw the distant columns of rain fall on the Sperrins and Glenhull. Further on I was sure that to the south, faint as old willow patterns on a plate, the Mournes showed. Even Slieve Gullion. Right or wrong my heart quickened.

Then I had foot trouble and stopped to pack my boots with roadside grass – a trick I had had to resort to over the years. I fell in with a tall, well-dressed man and asked him if he had heard of the old Fair of Orritor. He said he was a native of the place but never had and added: 'And if I may be so forward I would think by your southern accent you're not Protestant.'

The next man I met told me I was six miles out of Cookstown and seemed to think I was mad. Further on another man thought I might get 'dry-shod to Greencastle, but it's as much as you will. It'll be a slash.' Lightning jigged among the dark distant cloud and the thunder rumbled. But so far no rain. The sun went. I decided to thumb every car which passed, and there were few.

Two passed – three – a fourth, which suddenly pulled up. It was a priest driving alone. He was going through Greencastle but would have to make stops on the road; I didn't mind. We still had almost ten miles to go. The rain was moving its columns closer.

The priest, not young, drove with a Rosary entwined in his fingers, while in a pocket on the dashboard lay a row of smoking pipes; he was already smoking another. I had known and served Mass for a priest in Dromintee, an avid smoker. I looked at him closely. Incredible! It was the same, older certainly; a Father McKeever then in Arboe. I told him who I was and why I was in Tyrone and we swopped talk of people he had known.

(There had been the parish priest, a real cattle-man from Ardee, who had shot this priest's two goats with a faulty gun for which he had no licence either!)

A few people worked feverishly at hay in the fields, aware of the impending spill of rain. The priest disapproved. Near the townland of Formil we came upon a party working close enough to the road for him to shout as he slowed down:

'No luck in it . . . No luck in it . . . '

I saw the grins of the workers, saw them prepare to wave back (for this was after all a traditional jibe) but once they spotted the clerical collar they froze. We had time to see them stare at one another, stunned, perplexed. I wondered if this incident would take its furtive place in folklore if any misfortune or distress befell the workers in the natural course of events. I speculated and could hear a voice: 'One time one Sunday they were makin' hay when a priest told them they'd never have an hour's luck . . . So you see . . . '

Long after I had ceased to act as altar boy I was at Mass in Dromintee at Slieve Gullion. Father McKeever was the celebrant. During the collection men and youths went outside to chat and smoke (to evade the sermon) according to whatever priest was saying the Mass. Father McKeever was known to smoke himself during this interlude, but everyone was careful to avoid him nevertheless. He appeared suddenly in his vestments. Everyone bolted like hens before a strange cat, some standing where they were, myself among these: though I was not a smoker then. Three young men dashed through the gate, over a stone ditch and disappeared in tall bracken towards the bog. The priest ran calling:

'Stop! – Stop! – Or I'll leave you riding on a ragweed.'

He was no doubt taking advantage for spiritual purposes of the tenets of folk belief, but the boys didn't stop.

He left me off in Greencastle in the downpours.

23 Heinrich Wagner and The Gaelic Speakers

Assisted mainly by the ever-helpful aid of Michael Morris of Carnanransy I made a survey of the surviving Gaelic speakers – who numbered about forty – as well as writing up the social history of the decay of the language in Munterloney, its characters and general folklore.

Then came a letter from Heinrich Wagner, M.A., PH.D., Zurich, Switzerland, attached at the time to The Institute for Advanced Studies in Dublin. He had read my reports, and having consulted a few people in Dublin who had done inquiry in the area for songs and folk-tales only (Eamonn O'Toole had written a book of tales on Munterloney) he wrote doubting that the people enumerated could be genuine native speakers: they must be immigrants from Donegal who had settled there.

A brief knowledge of the economy of Munterloney would have revealed how ridiculous was such a supposition. I knew they were genuine natives of the area. The fact was that my predecessors on their exclusive quests for tales had ignored or overlooked such people as Padraig McCullagh and Michael Morris, comparatively young men in that era, and speakers I had found and checked in areas as far apart as Creggan in The Black Bog near Carrickmore to men like John Carolan and the old Treacy sisters in Glenelly.

Wagner accepted my assurance and wrote asking if he could find accommodation in Glenhull 'for a few days'. This was found in McCullagh's who owned the mill: Wagner came and stayed three weeks. His linguistic quest, coldly scientific as the folk quest, was to have some hilarious sidelines.

Padraig McCullagh, Michael Morris, Annie McCrae and Francis Frank Jack gave good information, everything very respectful. Then we went to look up Peter Pat Roe Bradley of Glenlark. Peter was crossing to his home, still in the familiar attire of army tunic covered with the sack, carrying some potatoes or turf in another sack. He tried to run when he spotted us. I advised Wagner to call to him in Irish, which he did, and Peter halted at once. Shyly he leaned against the ditch, plucking at stems of grass as he answered Wagner until finally I persuaded him to go inside, although I had warned Wagner of the state of the house, but he didn't mind.

There was still no fire although Peter tried to light one. We had brought a few bottles of stout from the pub at Gorticashel and these were drunk. The approach here was different than my own, less casual, more direct, plain question and answer. It went on for hours. Peter naturally wanted to know what 'part' Wagner had come from and when he was told, Switzerland, he laughingly refused to believe it, averring that Wagner had been 'born, bred and reared in some part of Ireland'. And that as well he must be Catholic.

(Later, when Annie McCrae asked if Wagner was a Catholic – which I didn't know – I diplomatically edged around the point: she would have been horrified to know she had recited old Catholic prayers to anyone other than a good Papish!)

We left when dusk was thickening into a sullen darkness. Peter came, very affably now, to the road. Appointments had been made for future meetings in Glenhull; but when Wagner checked Peter's full name and address he let a sort of quick, low cry and said lamentingly:

'Ah ... that means you're not comin' back ... '

Peadar Haughey's in the great peat-land of Creggan was a known centre for Gaelic enthusiasts. His farm was really an oasis amid the heather and turf, where he lived with one son and his wife Catherine. Then over eighty years old he had been very ill.

His wife Catherine was in the street as we came up, a woman badly bent by rheumatism although she continued to do domestic and household chores in and outside the house. She was wearing a sack apron, a kerchief on her head, and the usual agreeable expression despite her affliction. Wire-netting over the half-door kept out the marauding fowl. Behind it Peadar's face appeared, pale but full of verve, as he heard us greet his wife – in Gaelic from Wagner.

At once they exchanged greetings: at once the wire-netting was slammed down. His hand came out as if he were greeting a neighbour. His wife came along and added her share. The kitchen was clean and airy, tidy too, apart from the buckets and pots near the door, a not uncommon sight in the rural Ireland then beginning to discard and adapt. There was a bed for Peadar in the kitchen though not a 'Cooltyee': a single iron bed. Despite our protests Catherine immediately set to make tea. Already Wagner and Peadar were at work on the long, detailed questionnaires.

Then it began again. Amid a chore Catherine would say to Wagner:

'An' are you long home? An' will you stay long?'

Neither could accept the fact that a man so fluent in idiomatic Gaelic could have come from anywhere except Ireland and they were convinced that he was merely working in Switzerland.

A further interlude amused me immensely. Wagner had asked how he should explain himself to people where he thought it essential; I advised him to say he was a school-master: most of the people who came to houses like Haughey's were school-teachers anyway. This they could understand. But Wagner, although in bare head, wore a dark grey suit. When the inevitable question came up he either forgot what I had advised, refused to lie even in a good cause, or disdained to resort to mild subterfuge.

'What's this you said you were?' he was asked.

'I'm a student.'

I saw them both start – stare at that clerical grey – and fall into a silence. To them and most people in the area the term 'student' denoted a novice in Maynooth Catholic Seminary where no other colour was permitted except plain black. I could see no way at the moment out of the impasse, or was too amused; but it passed: Peadar's enthusiasm for a chance to converse in Gaelic surmounted any inherited or impulsive religious prejudices.

I had been told that 'Peadar was a going boy in his day' but was not altogether prepared for his quota of risqué anecdote and equivocal line, though I had often heard these at countless firesides. Age was admittedly affecting him, and he was repeating himself, and of course some tales were naive. Wagner had never run into his type of character before anyhow.

'Hoigh Catherine,' he might call when his wife had laboriously made her way outside to attend to fowl or something. He waited for her answer at the door. Then he would call: 'What's the Irish for your breast? This man wants to know.'

'Ah, sure,' she'd answer patiently, unflurried or annoyed, 'you know more about it than me.'

There were several such interludes even involving his son and a girl at work in the fields.

Towards evening Catherine asked me to bring the tea in a basket where her son was at harvest work helped by a neighbouring girl. I was glad to save her a chore, to save the son from coming from his work. He was used to strangers visiting his father; and while they ate I plaited the South Armagh brand of Harvest Knot, which they had never seen before; then mowed with the scythe, lifted and tied my sheaves, making the harvest band or binding of our country – which prevents the grain in the binding from germinating in prolonged bad weather – and this they had not seen either. The young man thanked me for bringing the tea, but apologised for 'putting the journey on me'. I knew they were a bit put about by my idiomatic work-phrases, use of vernacular, the mowing and the binding and the job I had explained I was doing.

(Twenty years later, living alone, that same young man was found murdered in that solitary house in Creggan bog.)

The first words I heard when I returned was Peadar saying:

'Ah, but I miss that neighbour of mine. Since he went to his rest there's not a livin' soul outside the walls of this house fit to talk to me in Irish now . . .'

I left Wagner and Peadar. We were using bicycles. Out in the bogland I had the curious feeling of being marooned, although down the road two scarlet-painted petrol-pumps stood like effigies. They only seemed to underline the mood of loneliness. A car sped by, into the wind, the sound of its exhaust snarling as the breezes mangled the roar on its flight across the heather.

After collecting in Glenelly we went again to Glenlark, but to the lower road to a family named McRory: all vouched for as genuine along with Mary Helen Devlin by Padraig McCullagh and Michael Morris.

This was the townland of Leaghan. I didn't know the house, had never even been up the old road, where a derelict forge stood at the bottom. Near the first thatched house, set low under the road, we met a little man stinking of turf smoke; his face brown and shrewd, the eyes almost Asiatic. I signalled to Wagner to speak: he did: the little man laughed, wheeled and said in English that he 'had as much Irish as would do him'. Suddenly he leaped over a stone ditch where he tried to turn a young heifer by booting her savagely on the hooves, then began to build a gap of stones. And then – how I never knew – he seemed to disappear somewhere like the fairy-man of legend. Looking to see where he had gone into concealment I was directly over the house, actually looking down the maw of the chimney below the level with the road. I distinctly heard a brief reference to us – who might we be – and then the talk turned into shrill Gaelic.

A laneway sloped past one gable. I went down, waiting for the charge of a dog. There was none. From the door of the house smoke oozed over a clabbery threshold; the door itself had been lifted off its hinges and placed lengthways over the threshold as a wind-shield in an effort to minimise the 'reek'. The smoke continued to come out like a vapouring paste squeezed from a tube by uncouth, erratic fingers.

Only then did I notice that a woman stood on a high dunghill across the street from the door. She began to shriek.

'There's no Irish here. Be off. We're all Irish here but we have no Irish an' want no Irish . . . '

I was flabbergasted. How did she know what we were after? And then I heard the swift chattering voice of our little dark man inside – but how the hell had he got in without our spotting the way?

'Away you go,' screamed the woman on the dunghill, waving her arms. She was in a nondescript array of dress, worn and patched, layer upon layer with the shortest outside, her grey hair loose and flying, a terrifying figure. Glenlark and the cynical gurgle of the river below . . . Life visibly petering out . . .

I was thunder-struck as well as embarrassed, looked round for Wagner but couldn't see him, and was about to 'make myself scarce' when another woman appeared. She was younger than the one on the dunghill though possibly in her seventies.

The second woman, also poorly dressed and in tatters seemed to trundle out of the doorway through the smoke, then to shoot or project herself right across the street, the smoke wafting behind her. She came up to me wraithed in the smoke and stinking of the 'reek' even worse than the little dark man who now remained inside. She was smaller in build than the woman on the dunghill who was now shrieking at the second woman as well as at me. The second woman looked back at her but said nothing. She wore a head-dress like the crown on an old black felt hat and her eyes appeared to be scalded from the smoke.

I began to talk to her as she went past and she swung round to a stop as if my speech had tethered her. I was now in a situation as bad as could be and decided to play this approach bluntly.

'Dammit, woman,' I began, 'you're bound to have Irish.' Hadn't I heard her up the maw of the chinmey . . . !

'Only a little,' she admitted.

This reply sent the woman on the dunghill into a frenzy of speech and hysterical gesture.

'I know songs,' cried the second woman as if hoping to allay the passion of the woman on the dunghill while trying to be truthful in reply to me at the same time. Her manner of voice, declamatory, yet with appeal made me ashamed of myself. She said something else before contrition flummoxed me, again with declamatory delivery which this time dropped to a hard, rustic chant.

'Songs . . . ?' I was trying to remember something. McCullagh had mentioned that Eamonn O'Toole had been up here collecting songs. Involuntarily I cried to her:

'Bejasus then you must be Jane Williams – Jane MacCrory,' I corrected.

'I am.' She plucked at my arm. 'Come on out to the barn' – in that chant she had. 'That Americee woman doesn't like to hear the Irish. She's me sister. She should have drowned in the river below. Come on. I have songs.'

(Her sister had been an emigrant many years back but was still sensitive to the jibes and jeers of Irish in America who equated the language and the Gaelic speaker, even among their own, with standards of low intelligence, social backwardness and ignorance, a verbal emblem which an inferiority complex compelled them to treat with derision and contempt.)

I introduced her to Wagner who stood waiting on the road. A stone flag like a bridge or *kesh* over the deep drain between house and road led to a door in a loft over a barn revealing how the little man had disappeared. Inside, the place was bare except for some rushes and a ladder lying on its side along one wall. We sat on the ladder which several times almost shot from under us, I converting into vernacular some of the questions which Wagner asked in English and needing an answer in Gaelic. The place got really cold, for there was a second door and wind through the open door edged the rushes back the way a tide edges seaweed on a beach.

Amid the talk and querying Jane kept apologising, saying it was cold, that 'the reek was bad,' and was critical of her brother and sister, and said that only for the reek she would make tea for us.

'It's terrible,' she said, 'to have strangers comin' an' goin' away from a place without a drop of tea.'

The cold defeated us, and in the end Wagner arranged to have her brought down to Glenhull along with Peter Pat Roe.

Further on we met a woman carrying a rope over her arm, two dead hens in one fist and a table-knife in the other. A dog trotted by her side. Pointing to the hens I asked her what she would call them in Irish. She knew alright: she was Mary Helen Devlin. At once herself and Wagner engaged in a lively conversation. She walked on. Near a 'pipe' or drain she calmly dropped the two dead hens into the river.

'A poor sort of price I'd get for them,' was all the comment she made. The dog hopped over the ditch to smell after the hens and she rattled off a shrill rebuke at it in Gaelic. The dog cowered, shrank, and came back to the road.

I knew that the knife had bled the hens and they were being cast off with 'all bad luck go with them' in the hope that their ailment would not infect others in the flock.

In those weeks none of us thought of bed before 2.00 in the morning.

24 The Break

There is a tale of the man who said he was too busy to be ill. Nevertheless, despite the smoke and the wide-open door in a house unopened for two years none of us got as much as a simple cold.

But Alice felt some strain and repeatedly told me I was working too hard. When the next collection went in, each getting bigger than the other, I was advised to stop for a month, go home, take a rest. Alice actually looked transformed. We would go back this time to her home place in Faughart on the Louth-Armagh border and stay with her mother. And still I was reluctant to leave: there was material to collect and it was flowing. Supposing people closed their minds to me. And then realising just how obsessively absorbed I had become in the quest I frightened myself.

The shutters went back on the windows. Into Omagh – Alice's first visit since she had come through in the previous December two weeks before Christmas. The weather was good. Both of us now were inwardly but immaturely excited. But we said nothing. On to the Derry train going towards Dungannon and Portadown. The stretches of bog-land with a view of the peaty plain of Creggan and the distant hills with the peaks of the Sperrins behind, were no longer simply wilderness. For the first time we seemed to understand exactly what we had done and were doing out there. Though impersonal no longer, ages of Time might have elapsed since that December day when we had arrived: as in a sense ages had elapsed in reverse: I had been reeling them back in many minds, involving us in the events of people I had never met and never would, dead some of them before we had been born; but known to us like relatives in tale, account and story preserved in the minds of their descendants.

Yet it sounded and seemed unreal: there was some spirit about it I couldn't label and pin down. I think I felt at once like a deserter as well as interpreter. From Portadown on to the Dublin train taking us to Dundalk. We talked little, didn't need to speak our thoughts. Expression would sound crazy, naive, ridiculous. Was it really only a dream . . . ? Glenhull . . . the nights of talk and memory eluding the smother of Time, secreting itself in the minds of strangers who were strangers to me no longer. How could one put this sensation into feasible words . . .

Does the dedicated folklore-collector sell his soul as well . . . ?

We were rescued from incoherent fantasy-flung thought by a commonplace happening that could not make sense. Yet it was so madly exhilarating that even to this day we can recapture the thrill.

The train had entered the first of the rock cuttings over Newry. We were back in South Armagh. ('A stone in Glenhull? If they found a stone they'd put it on the mantelpiece and call the neighbours,' my landlord had said.) The comradeship, the kinship of rock and stones, the warmth in the ring of mountains – over Cloghogue and the Mosque-like dome of the church – into the cut-blocks or rock at the famous Wellington Cutting, where the Ghost Train used be seen near Ayalloghue before Republicans derailed a troop train following the opening of the Ulster Parliament in 1921 . . . I was in home country. We might have been two people released from prison. On hurtled the train. We used to time our work schedule by trains such as this. Good God – I had never been on a train through our own valley in my life before! No reason why I should. Slieve Gullion – Faughil – the old dance-hall on the hillside empty and derelict – the Rebel cobbler Casey's wee cabin, dead as himself beyond in Dromintee, buried under the National flag to the piping of an Irish Lament – The Gap of the North where the Ulster Plantation was really decided – Moyry Castle built by Mountjoy, still acting as a sentry on a border – Faughart beyond the cutting with the tuft of trees in the graveyard surmounting the gentle hill – the wide, flat warm acres. We were saying things we don't remember in ejaculations and passengers stared, smiled or smirked and wondered where we had dropped from.

I could have truthfully said from a long lost world. I was now in the country of The Tain with the hills of Cooley on my left. The Dead of the Sperrin Foothills had risen and spoken to me through the dim recesses of forgotten corners of living minds. I had waded in the sagas.

McGuill's on The Big Bridge in Dundalk; never missed a drink there with Joe and Frank and Annie on Saturday nights. The whole bar modernised; not a snug or piece of brown solid wood in sight. It steadied me: I saw: I knew what was happening now and what I was doing and why.

We spent a month at Faughart and around Dundalk and Slieve Gullion. But couldn't adjust. I began to collect more folklore from my mother-in-law. We returned to Glenhull, calmer but still excited. I was thoroughly surprised to find I felt I was returning 'home'.

Alice hadn't minced words. The glen and the environs scared her, but this drawback was more than compensated for by the warm-hearted hospitality and dignity of the people.

I had one shutter off when my first visitor arrived, Francis McBride. He shook our hands vigorously to welcome us back and had brought a gift of eggs and milk. Mal McAleer came next with more gifts of eggs, as well as a full bucketful of spring water from the wee well far up the road. Francis Daniel came pedalling on his bike: all with the same traditional welcome. We got stout and a drop of 'the craythur' in McCrae's and the house was full of other visitors as soon as darkness fell.

25   A Tale of Two Typewriters

Following Wagner's visit the journalists discovered me, quoted me without seeing me, talked of my getting material from 'all creeds and classes' (which, taking the sweeping phrase calmly, was true, though I had not said so: one Presbyterian tradition bearer took particular pains to show me the site on his land of a Mass Rock. His father had been one of the old Gaelic speakers.) There was the usual reactions I had feared – some pique, some open resentment, some fear that what had been told to me in confidence would next appear in print. I spent most of a month allaying alarm and re-establishing myself in the confidence of my narrators. Only Francis Daniel remained withdrawn, claimed he had no more stories except one called 'The White Bird of The Lowlands' but couldn't remember it.

I needed a typewriter and another table and chair. In Omagh I was directed to an auctioneer's rooms by Paddy Bogues, then producing amateur drama in Omagh. In the rooms I met a partner of the firm; a stocky-built sandy-haired man, young enough, with a calm expression and a soft resonant voice. He did not have what I wanted but remarked that at a coming auction he believed some typewriters were to be offered.

When I told him where I was living he explained he knew the house; had been there at a house-warming dance when it had been built. But why there? He knew I was not a native.

When I explained he was more than interested, knew of me though not in Glenhull. He was an amateur actor himself, although I had to confess I had never heard of him though I had heard of The Omagh Players under Paddy Bogues.

The auctioneer-partner was Paddy McAlliney: Munterloney would indeed be his ancestral territory. He later joined the Group Theatre Company in Belfast under Harold Goldblatt and took the part of The Slab Fallon in my own play: *Dust Under Our Feet* both in Belfast and London from which he and others of the cast went into films while Murphy returned to his folklore collecting and glad to do so.

(Coincidence became more the rule than the exception during my stay in Glenhull. With Michael Morris I went to a Charley Conway's near Greencastle to meet a storyteller, and together we crossed a single-plank footstick over a swollen river. Neither of us knew the flood had cracked it the day before. Nor was our storyteller there. But in the talk as to where I had come from Charley discovered that a first cousin of mine, Jimmy Farmer, born and reared in Birkenhead, had met and married a sister of Charlie's in New York.)

The auction was announced though not under the aegis of McAlliney's firm. It was held on a wet day in a huge shed in Omagh. My old machine had already typed over a million words of folklore in Glenhull, the platen worn, the draw-band when it broke I repeatedly repaired with ordinary boot rivets and the spring from an old clock.

I met Paddy Bogues and explained my errand. He too was looking for a typewriter for a friend. There were several on offer. I selected one which happened to be the machine he had his eye on. He suggested an arrangement. He would buy a worn though still serviceable desk machine and expected to get it cheap. He would then try to buy the portable: if it exceeded the figure he was prepared to pay I was to give him the nod. I agreed. I had never been at such an auction before anyway.

He bought the big desk machine as he had hoped and called out the name:

'Murphy. From Glenhull.'

Near me a voice repeated in wonderment:

'Glenhull? . . . A typewriter . . . ?'

The portable machine went up, the bidding exceeded Bogues' figure, I acknowledged his nod and he bought it as well, again calling out my name, which the auctioneer of course repeated in full voice:

'Murphy. Glenhull.'

Again that voice whispered in awe:

'Two bluddy typewriters . . . ? Glenhull?'

I also bought a chair and a table, all to be called out: 'Murphy. Glenhull.'

A week later I was in Omagh to pay my rent. Dan McCrae had a story for me. There had been gossip all week in the town about 'Someone from Glenhull in the mountains beyond Gortin who bought two typewriters and a chair and table.' Dan claimed that Paddy Bogues had confirmed the story but said he didn't know the man, would give no detail or explanation. Dan like others assumed that Bogues was playing one of the pranks for which he was noted. For Dan, who knew why I was in Glenhull without apparently understanding the quest in full context, said he wouldn't believe a word of it.

'Now who in the name of heaven out at Glenhull would buy one typewriter let alone two?'

I told him I had. He seemed to be amazed.

(Years later in Warrenpoint on Carlingford Lough, still after folklore, I met a bank cashier who hearing that I had been in Glenhull said he had been in Omagh for some time. He asked me if I had ever heard the story of the man from Glenhull who once bought two typewriters at an auction in Omagh. Surely there couldn't be a word of truth in it. Not unless the poor man was mad. Out in Glenhull . . . ? Had I met him?

I replied that I had indeed met the man. Did I know him? More truthfully than I realised at the time I said no; I didn't know him too well at all . . . Not as well as I thought anyhow.

26 A Man of Stones

With McBride and Michael Morris and young Frank Morris we cycled to Glenelly. At almost every house of the way, turn of road Morris could tell something of the people, some event, as in Barnes where a bishop in late Penal times had confirmed his flock. We talked religion and philosophy in the teeth of a stiff breeze. Talk in the North proper can become too preoccupied with the religious thing.

Glenelly, which Morris claimed was the longest in Ireland, extended sixteen miles from The Six Towns near Ballinascreen to The Plum or Plumbridge and Newtownstewart. It is certainly one of the most striking, even dramatic. On the side of the summit of the mountain turf banks showed like a graph. They talked of work 'in the Moss' when they remembered it 'black with people' and no one wearing boots: in fact even around Glenhull old Annie McCrae and other women and even girls returned from emigration rarely wore shoes 'around the house'.

We visited the holy well in Badoney and noticed the usual votive offerings – pins, rags and coppers strewn about or lying at the bottom of the water. (One evening later on cycling through I saw a beggarman with sleeve rolled up retrieving the coppers; when he spotted me he snatched off his cap, joined his hands and pretended to pray.)

There was Sperrin and the mid-road commons where a Fair used be held opposite Carleton's pub. White houses nestled in far flung dips and hollows all along the range, some of which I knew.

Heading for The Six Towns we skirted the confines of Broughderg nearer Glenhull. ('I never believed to find such wild desolation in Tyrone,' a Donegal journalist told me once in Omagh.) Yet, with its strips of arable land there was a mood of hope about Broughderg compared to the shrinking despair in Glenlark. We passed women under shawls going to the church. Morris stopped to ask one a question; she told some lore and invited us to call some night. She held a Rosary entwined in her fingers. Her companion held a prayer-book bulging with leaflets and Memory Cards.

In The Six Towns near Ballinascreen we hoped to meet the man of the stones: George Barnett. He was old then but active, a self-taught geologist whose opinions and comments were respected in academic centres in Ireland and England. A friend of Morris's, James O'Hagan (the first man to tell me a story about the ghost of a horse) said George was on the mountains with his sack and chipping hammers. No one could tell when he might return; on his way back he might make a late ceili in any house.

We rode into Ballinascreen, one of the most delightful village-towns imaginable, delicately set with the mountains not too close, not too far away. Planter-built as 'Draperstown' it was the centre of the O'Cahan country, full of history, of lore and scholarship, with memories of a famous, wild Fair.

Word came to us hurriedly that Barnett had been seen making for his home. We retraced as fast as we could.

Barnett lived alone in a two-storied slated house not too well attended to outside. Small, lightly-built he looked and was clad like an easy-going farmer. He carried a sack on one shoulder, greeted everyone, shook hands, was introduced to me, gave me the welcome and invited us inside.

The kitchen was in the familiar farm-house style with dresser, plain table, chairs and stools, the hearth at the floor level: it was beautifully paved with round stones smoothed by water action, the first of this type I had seen. A long crook hung down from the crane. He said he must make tea, ignored our protests, and carried on.

Where he had dumped his sack I don't know. I knew it contained chippings of rock or boulder. There was hardly room for any more in the house. The table – mantelpiece – windows – dresser-ledges and shelves: all were packed with stones he had chipped. Preparing the table for the tea he swept the stones into a pile. None was labelled. He picked up a piece, enumerated its mineral content, then gave its geological history and where it had come from. Suddenly down to the room – where I saw nothing else except stone-laden tables, boxes and chairs – he brought up another piece and explained. Uranium. Again nothing bore a label to help the identification.

Carelessly tossing the stone aside he began to light the fire. The hearth was clean, cold and black. He set up turf clods on their edges. (At night in Glenhull a properly set turf fire burned exactly for a definite period of time; no clock consultation was needed.) From outside he dragged in butt first a huge hawthorn, remarking that it was a Lone Thorn and that he expected Fairy company that night. The butt he set amid the turf. He filled a kettle and swung it down. Then he got a can of paraffin oil, slashed it on, threw in a lighted match and the whole fireplace exploded in flame and roared like a furnace. All the time he talked. When the fire subsided he sloshed on more oil and if the white vapour wriggled like a wraith tossed in a lighted match. Again the burst and boom of the flame. In the end turf, bush butt and coal caught fire and burned without the aid of oil. The kettle began to sing.

After we had taken tea amid the stones banked to the back of the table he took down his fiddle. He had some lore, but had such a puckish sense of humour that it was dangerous to use his material. His fiddle-bow was a long tapering rod which he claimed he also cut from a Fairy Thorn, and would pause to remind us that much of the quality of the music he produced was due to the benign influence of the fairies because of the origin of the bow.

But he understood the nature and purpose of the work I was doing, laid his puckish humour aside, and gave us good accounts from the lore of the area. He regretted he had forgotten much tradition which he now regarded as more essential than ever.

Abruptly he then requested us to view his latest interest. Elaborate and intriguing stone circles had been found under six feet of turf in a bog at Beaghmore not too far away. Barnett, having studied this, contended that the positioning of the stones, much like Stonehenge, was designed to provide a calendar from seed to harvest for primitive man. He had slept out in Beaghmore to mark the position of the first light of the sun and shadow on the stones, annotated each, until every stone had relative meaning. From a diagram he re-erected the position of the standing stones in his garden with stakes as a replica of Beaghmore and began a more minute checking. He had a long chart of explanations. It all seemed intriguing and complicated until he began to explain. The TV people were to have done a film not so long ago, but Barnett had suddenly died.

He used to send for me when he had recollected some item of tradition, or had found a man on the northern side of the Sperrins with folklore to tell. It was late when I got home that night. Alice was in a state of shock. Patrick had fallen down the steps at the gate and split his head.

27 A Killing on The Road to Rome

So far the family had enjoyed good health and escaped serious knocks and falls. The river was close, and deep six-feet drains or sheughs along the road were a menacing worry. Now and then one had to haul out a man in his cups, take him in and clean him up, drench him with black tea, and set him on his way: some were quiet, some grateful, some nasty and these I ordered out, drain or not.

From the Commission Sean O'Sullivan sent me a cutting from a Dublin evening newspaper. It told how I had killed a woman on a highway in Italy in May on the road to Rome.

Around that time in Glenhull I had received a registered letter re-directed from Dromintee in South Armagh. There were five 'Michael Murphy's' in Dromintee, my father being one, but I was the only one with a 'J' wedged between: a point which always irritated my mother, because it had been stuck there by a godparent, a Welsh-woman in Liverpool named Jones, and whom I never remember seeing. I dropped the 'J' until my schoolmaster, Patrick Hearty, had it restored.

The letter inside was in a language I couldn't read except for one word 'studio' which I associated with radio, never then having got as far as a TV or film set. It was in Italian as I was told when I sent the letter to the Commission for translation. The letter told me that the writer was an Italian lawyer nominated by the State to act for me in my absence as defender in a lawsuit against me for having run down a woman with my car on the highway at a place called Sarzana on the Aurelian highway. I had never been to Italy in my life and had never driven a car let alone possess one.

I was advised what to do and told not to worry once I had confirmed where I had been in May. I had by then a fair good idea as to by whom and how my name had been used and replied to the lawyer as directed. I felt strongly at the time about the illegal misuse of my name, but the mood passed amid the welter of collecting folklore and I had forgotten all about the matter until the news-cutting arrived.

The man who had impersonated me had been sentenced in his absence at

Spezia, Italy to eight months imprisonment. Murphy had tried to overtake a bus in his car and had run down a motor-cycle combination, killing the woman and injuring the man severely, the woman's son.

I had been out all day and got the letter only when I arrived in late evening. I was of course hopping mad. To assuage the mood I went to McCrae's pub, which was rarely open until nightfall (whatever about official closing hour – the nearest police barracks anyhow was eight miles away at Dunamore.)

Here I met two characters conversing about Crumlin Road Jail. One, ignoring episcopal decree, had just been released after serving a sentence for poteen-making: a big cumbersome fellow with awkward hands: yet I had seen those hands play lively fiddle music for us one night in Francis Daniel's. They talked.

'What was it like in quod?'

'Not so bad. Hard labour be damned: work in a garden: you'd do more labour for one day "In the Moss" at turf-cutting. A good bed. No planks,'– And he added solemnly:

'I even got to a concert in it. An' a picther show.'

He meant films.

'An' I'll hold you you weren't at one since?'

'Aw, divil the one. An' won't till I get back I suppose.'

Incidental gossip was proving the quick run-down on local social history, however unflattering the implication of the levels; but at least this instance restored my humour.

So squatting on upturned cases of stout in a circle around a hissing oil-heater, like devotees of some esoteric alcoholic rite, we stayed and drank, served ourselves, told folklore, paid McCrae as one of the circle, though he drank none, talked and, of course, heard more folklore. All in the darkness except for the glow from the reflector of the oil-heater.

28 Following Fairies Further A-Field

A young American Army officer, home from the wars, had brought his aged father to Glenhull which he had left at the age of sixteen. His name was John McGurk. Though politely indulgent he was not interested – to put it mildly – in my work until I explained its innate purpose and the scientific and cultural ends for which the work was being done: working in the present on products and presentation of the past for purposes of the future. He was a little surprised to know that I understand the sinister connotation for instance of such terms as 'fairy' for homosexual in the States. (Years back in South Armagh our Pahvees enlightened us on the dual meanings of such terminology, while whiskey-jar rolls of American papers made us familiar with the event and general argot of the Roaring Twenties!)

McGurk insisted on driving me and my guides around the countryside on the quest especially on Sundays. We would approach a house with McBride and Morris in the car. They knew the houses well.

'Begod she'll be wipin' the biss out of her eyes now. She'll have seen the car comin'.'

' "Oh dear Lord" – in paraphrase – "who is the quality comin' to us now? Redd the house –" '

' "Give the floor a wipe of the besom." '

' "Lift that oul' shirt off the chair – Put the things away . . ." '

And so on. Some women came to the half-door, hand shading the eyes before bolting back into the kitchen.

We went to Carrickmore. Sheila Campbell, who had been a correspondent of The Commission, came with her sister to show us Relig na mBan: The Woman's Graveyard where no living woman and no dead man may enter; neither of the girls would cross the low sod ditch into the tiny cemetery set amid pasture lands. Its origin was attributed to another manifestation of the fiery temper of Columbcille (whose stone beds were also in the area) in which he cursed to death a woman who had accused him of being the father of her child. She was first to be buried there.

Back to Glenelly to meet another American, younger than McGurk's father, but who had also left at the age of sixteen and was seeing his home place for the first time. (They said he was like the man who had seen the murder of the bank-cashier Glass in Newtownstewart by the police inspector Montgomery. No witnesses could be produced at the trial but there had been one: a youth from Glenelly. When he fled home and told what he had seen he was immediately packed off to the States or Australia next day from Derry.)

He hated the place and in the fields amused us and made young McGurk sardonic: youthful impressions failed to live up to expectations and he said he would go back next day if he could get a berth. Out in the fields the cow-manure appalled him. To old McGurk he'd cry:

'The God-damned cow-muck, Pop – Don't stand in it. God dammit, Pop – Everywhere – More of it there by Christ – Look, Pop. Wait, Pop. Watch it.' By then he was himself standing to the ankles in a full-sized cow-clap which squelched dark-green liquid manure over the two-toned shoes and the light-coloured low-hanging trouser-ends. He 'hollered' when he noticed. Less than a week later he had got that berth and was on his way back to the States.

There was also a Fair in Gortin. One summer fair was known as 'The Girls' Fair' at which match-making tentatively began.

My father came down and went back again as well: the loneliness of the place disturbed him he said; as it was now beginning to disturb Alice: like the fleeing American in reverse she refused to go to a local town unless when absolutely necessary. Disturbed I knew what I had to do: collect twice as hard: or else prepare to stay on my own.

McGurk drove me to Belfast to do a few talks. Out of one of these the BBC asked would it be possible to find enough material on Fairy Lore to present in depth one thirty-minute programme; I was to go around the

North to unearth narrator and material, later to be followed by a recording van. I could provide enough to fill such a programme for a week. (Six were finally produced which so revealed the unknown world of Fairy that a Belfast newspaper actually wrote an editorial about the discovery in their backyard!)

The break would be welcome; Alice encouraged it: the money would be handy. But she would be alone: Brigid O'Hare was working in England and my father had taken ill. The memory of Patrick hastily swathed in a sheet, his head pouring blood, while she hurried with two children to a phone in the post-office leaving Patrick lying alone was a shock that failed to wear off either of us.

And when she was asked if she had not 'Got an office' for the boy she was as puzzled as I was and when she understood what it was – she blew up. I was horrified.

It was a religious custom performed by the priest and validly canonical; but in Faughart (of St. Brigid) or in South Armagh we had never heard of its being practised. But people around Glenhull, as well as resorting to the wide range of folk cures which I had been noting, avoided calling medical aid and relied on the cures and a priest said to 'have a good Office'. To be ill was to reveal blemish, and blemish in the old days of clan demoted one.

There was one instance which had already stirred our social conscience, folk consideration or not, to express our attitudes. A local young man had become insane over an unrequited love affair. The curate courageously challenged him when he charged into the parochial house armed with some weapon. Then the young man broke down and cried that he had 'come for an Office.' People talked of the incident afterwards:

'I was up to Mass with him last summer, an' a finer an' a nicer boy you couldn't wish to meet.'

'... All his family died young: wouldn't it be a nice thing if he hada died young too if anythin' is to happen to his head...'

A third said: 'God will take care, I'm sure, that nothin' bad will come over him, an' settle him before he does any harm.'

We always associated that terribly poignant incident with another concerning Life itself. Alice was in old Annie McCrae's helping me ferret out detail on the folk section of conception and pregnancy. A local young woman came in, home from England where she had been married for some years. She had to tell that she had just one child. Old Annie remarked, significantly of course, that her school companion married at home already had six.

'Oh good God no...!' cried the young woman appalled.

So was old Annie – for a different reason. The young woman said that the glen was too lonely for her: wouldn't stay now for a 'car-load of gold.' And even shuddered at the idea of Alice with three boys.

Gossip again spot-lighting both the decay and upsurge of pulses in social norm and manner: no more big families: no stay in Ireland: not till she wakens up and provides the rurals with amenities of the urban and the sense of living, however false and tinselled, such as they get in England: blind reverence for folk practice and custom in deference to community attitude disintegrating, other reverences inevitably to be discarded.

I spent about three weeks travelling the North – the Mournes, Glens of Antrim, Strangford and Lough Erne – but made back to Glenhull as often as possible. I'd had to get the consent of the Folklore Commission of course. Professor Delargy had agreed providing the Commission got copies of all the discs to be cut later. As well I collected as much general lore as possible while sounding out intervening areas where concentrated inquiry might prove profitable to some collector in the future.

I had suggested a holiday while I was away. If Alice left she was afraid she might not return. I was terribly upset, but buried it under collecting and still more collecting.

Then she took ill and the gossips began again, but instead of infuriating us we remembered the folk mind and found it all amusing till we heard what the trouble was.

Her absence from the kitchen being noticed the talk started. A woman then came asking for us to collect buttermilk from the milk-man, a woman who had never called before. Unsuspecting we wondered why: because if one's churn was empty one should call on the neighbours to avoid affront before buying commercially. Even old Annie McCrae furtively roped us into this practise. Didn't want to impose. The old order was breaking up. Independence of individuality defying the communal concept of nothing concealed, share and share alike.

Milk was bought for the woman, and more milk – for a week. She collected surreptitiously. Then the cause of the itching curiosity was blurted out: wasn't Alice going to have a child? Hadn't so-and-so seen or heard or noticed – and wasn't she lyin' down a lot – for a week? And so on.

Just as bluntly Alice told the woman what she thought of the proposition of a confinement in an area as remote as Glenhull. The woman didn't want any more buttermilk. But in a few days I could find a sense of chill about the old people I worked with. We were back almost into the groove where the curate had set us the Sunday morning he had preached about Communism. Or, as one man had told me when he found me drenched on a road, we were bluddy pagans up in South Armagh and all half-mad anyway.

We had treated the temporary upset lightly as tiredness. Alice had strong fine teeth. An extraction of one in Cookstown continued to bleed so badly she needed medical attention. I cycled to Gortin in a heavy bitter rain for some medicine and found the bicycle lamp wouldn't work. When I got back to Glenhull I found she had had a recurrence of the haemorrhage which had attacked in the summer of '49 before Peter had been born. The doctor had to be recalled. He advised her to leave the glen when she had recovered.

The gossips naturally said it was really a miscarriage. The harassed, retreating, dwindling column of an old folk community was gratified and satisfied.

Only when she was recovering did Alice tell me the attack had occurred in the dark when she had been out to bring in turf from the shed on the road. She had had to crawl in, up the steps, up the path, up the high step into the house. The children went into a panic.

I decided we would leave as soon as she could: as soon as I could get a house back home. But she refused. I would finish my chore.

29 Tinker Trouble

I was too upset to work, even to write in the house. I had to stay and attend to Alice anyhow and look after the family. Neglected chores occupied my time, including a distempering job near the door.

I heard the people say that van-loads of Tinkers (as everyone called the Travelling People) had come on Sunday to the heath beside Formil Rock.

Next day they began to fan out.

Tinkers and Travelling People were part of the subject for folk research as well – families which regularly frequented an area, names, events, incidents and, of course, the *ceant*: Padraig McCullagh had helped much with this aspect. But the old women, and some men, dreaded them; aware of this fear the Travelling People imposed and profited accordingly.

People like Annie McCrae went in holy horror of 'their prayers' – meaning their curses – even their disfavour, of which the tribes were also very much aware to their benefit. The familiar folk solace was that 'I'd as soon have their prayers (cursings) as their blessin' if they prayed a potful on me.'

'Why don't you work?' someone said.

'I'll work in death,' answered the Travelling Woman.

I was distempering near the door, and clad for the job in old clothes, when the reconnaissance party reached our place: two young girls in brassy plaited hair, long tartan check skirts and boots to their calves. Each wore a shawl. Western verbal music capered through their speech; but I was in neither mood not humour – folklore notwithstanding – at that time for ingratiating myself with the tribes. They went, reported back of course, and the van appeared and stopped. There was a lone man, it appeared, in that house, not a native by his accent, hardly a policeman: a good mark, as our own pedlar Pahvees would say.

Out of the van came an old lassie clad like her younger brood, her face as dark as a wizening chestnut. She began the usual litany and I told her to go to hell and miles beyond it and Fiddler's Green as well. She looked at me.

She was bedecked with a string of tins as belligerent as a bandolier of bullets and carried a few tin cans as well; she smelled like a bag of wet rags. Again I told her I wanted neither her tins, her cans, her blessings. She thrust a shoulder forward, and began again, spreading saintly invocation for me and mine 'and the sick woman' (How the hell had she heard of that?) 'and my affairs in this world and the next.'

Maybe it was the betrayal of gossip which infuriated me. One naked knee showed through a slit in the old trousers. I deliberately ripped it further, pretending fierce anger. She flung some malediction at me that sounded like a blessing until you had to reflect. And then I remembered an old man with Gaelic in South Armagh noted for his repertoire of ancient Irish curses which grand old Gaelic speaking women like Mary Nugent of Slieve Gullion refused to relate above a whisper – and then not in full. But it included a line of baleful invective about 'The grey cat's kittlin' as Mary had translated it.

I didn't need the full version: I got no further than 'kittlin' (kitten) with the Travelling Woman. She winced, stared, then clapped her hands to her ears, turned away, muttering: ironic I suppose to think that aware of the fruits of imposition of their own cursing they were nevertheless afraid of mine and must have known it. One glare from the road – she even closed the gate, into the van and off.

The incident restored my humour as well as Alice's when I told her. That evening Michael Morris had another tale to tell.

His neighbour, Mickey Gillan, a good narrator of mine, lived alone. He had lost a leg and had, as the local phrase put it 'a stick leg.' He dreaded the Tinkers, knowing he could not thwart them in their plundering if they tried. He saw one group of men and women approach the loanan to his house. From the back window he crossed to the threshold, his stick in his hand. When they appeared he was facing the doorway, swearing in English and in Gaelic. He flung his cap on the doorstep and began to shout into the empty house. The Tinkers stopped in a group, watching.

Ignoring them Micky roared:

'Come out now you rotten whore's gett – Come out if you're a man an' I dare you walk on that cap. Walk over it I say an' I'll leave you a corpse across your own bleddy doorstep – Come out damn you if you're man enough – I'll split you to the navel – Come out an' be a man.'

The Tinkers fled. Assault and battery and near-murder among themselves was one day's work: witnessing murder among people not of the clans was a horse of a different colour.

30 Turn of The Year and The Naghan tuighe Mhuire.

A brief holiday at Blackrock outside Dundalk with friend-folklorist and able raconteur Tommy Hollywood and back to Glenhull. Illness had not quite dampened the earlier sensations but the masses of material had swamped me. Again the same welcome from the people.

But the weather was bad. From our doorway I watch Mullabolig mountain shake off sombre shadow while far away, like corroded supports in a furnace of fantasy, columns of rain deluged distant townlands miles beyond Gortin. Yet harvest magic was about. Men mowed with scythes until dusk, even to darkness. Jimmy O'Neill in his cabin in Allwollies across the Owenkillew periodically flushed his window with light as he doused his fire with paraffin oil.

In spring and in hay and harvest old men, and most women, may in body be confined to the kitchen or a chair at the fireside; but in spirit they are out in the fields. In bad weather leisure to reflect intensifies their concern more profoundly than the men and women actually engaged in the work. If they talk at all the speech is chopped, the memory langled. But I had to make my rounds to restore acquaintanceship at least. All of them had heard of my wife's illness, castigated the few gossips, and then said they had heard I might be leaving. At the time I had not yet made such a decision though I had thought about it: as I knew their minds they knew much of my own: we were rurals of the one kin.

My father came on a visit but curtailed it when an early layer of snow fell. I had now amended my plan of work. Research in the Munterloney territory had convinced me that I could spend at least ten years working hard without hoping to exhaust the complete potentialities of its folk heritage: after all Sean O'Sullivan's monumental *Handbook of Irish Folklore* was a questionnaire covering over 600 pages. So I would concentrate on as full a coverage as possible of the better narrators close at hand and with luck would have a fair conspectus of the lore by the time my two year contract had expired. The Commission then existed on a varying grant.

Padraig McCullagh had now quite accidentally – in his typically indifferent way of taking his knowledge for granted – revealed that he was a craftsman. In our house on a ceili he was explaining how ordinary rushes were once used locally to make, not only the usual farm-yard burden ropes, but as sets of riding and ploughing harness as well. This was exciting news: of straw and hay work I had known, but rushes . . . ! His explanation of the craft was so intricate however, and no doubt I so dense as well as worried, that he said off-hand:

'I'll make you a set and then you'll see for yourself.' And went on to talk of other crafts: the old Irish spade – he'd make one of those too: boot and clothes brushes made of horse-hair – he'd make a set.

Everyone was stunned.

His harness is the now famous *Naghan tuighe Mhuire,* as he called it (in folk-tale linked tenuously with The Virgin) since displayed by The National Museum as part of the Folk Life Section at The British Association meeting in Dublin.

I succeeded in finding him at home one wet day and to demonstrate the craft for me he finished a tug of the work. It was made of melled rushes alright. When he asked me to test it for strength I remembered the delicate rush (forgetting the folktale which moralises on 'Unity Being Strength' when a plaited rush is used) and tugged tentatively. Padraig Phelimy Laidir saw my hesitation, took it from me, wedged one end under his boot and pulled, then made me pull: as we said it would have held the 'Queen Mary' in dock. Delicately fashioned, expertly plaited and with leads ranging out of the main work like stems off a plant, he had produced a work of true art: an article which our forefathers regarded as a piece of ordinary use of local materials for practical purpose: a lesson to us and our age.

As they said he 'had hands for anything.' Yet craftsman as he was, his own house was almost a shambles (the shoemaker with bad boots, the smith's horse never fully shod, etc.) The fact was the man, then over 70, was over-worked. His chairs slewed when you sat on them. He didn't mind that a hen layed in his 'Cooltyee' bed in the kitchen: when she cackled he skelped her out with his cap. Once when he was clearing up work to come back with me to Glenhull one Sunday evening I saw him change from work attire.

Near the door sacks of flour and feeding meal sat on flat stones, which were familiar in earlier times; indeed to display this wealth proudly. Garments were tossed in a nondescript pile on top of an old-time chest in another corner. There was also a thin-staved sally-bound barrel near the door. He first washed himself in a bowl of water, holding it with one hand and using the other for the ablutions, drying himself with the first cloth his hand reached on top of the chest. Out of the barrel he next yanked his 'good Sunday suit' of navy-blue and went to the room to change.

His sister, unmarried like himself, a big and bulky woman and not in good health moved laboriously about the kitchen at chores, resting often on tables, though insisting on making tea; and while Padraig was outside attending to cattle sang some old ballads and folk songs while now and then hens flew to perch on the half-door.

Before we left that evening rain began slowly and struck the glass as if it were a sheet of transparent lead being scored by invisible chisels. His sister Mary Anne lighted a 'Sacred Heart lamp' with its red globe, not for votive purpose but as illumination.

I kept remembering one day I had met Padraig cycling from Gortin Fair. We had met on the top of the old mountain road six miles out of Gortin. He was clad in his usual garb including the old raincoat buttoned to his throat and was as excited as a schoolboy. Radio Eireann had sent him a cheque for his voluminous recordings in Gaelic and he hadn't expected to be paid, hadn't thought of money. He would return with me to Gortin to 'stand me a treat' and waved my protests aside. Back we went.

Like Francis Daniel McAleer, Padraig Phelimy was not a drinking man: if he consented to drink, his stout had to come out of the bottle to his mouth and he would drink as if eager to get it down and done with, without any obvious pleasure: it was a traditional act he must respect. In a bar-room full of men in Gortin, where a ballad-singer whined above his fistful of coloured offerings, I saw John Carolan of Glenelly among the men sitting on the long stools around the table. Then I was astonished to learn that while each had heard of the other they did not appear ever to have met. I introduced them. The rapture on McCullagh's face possibly out-shone that on Carolan's as Gaelic speech and exclamation and ejaculation in joy and wonder passed between them. A few men chipped in and with word or two, found themselves evidently swamped and then like everyone else sat to listen until finally they resumed conversation in English quietly among themselves. The voices of the others rang through the room. Padraig had completely forgotten not only 'the treat' but me as well. Half-an-hour and more later I left unnoticed. They were as engrossed as ever and still talking Gaelic.

31 Fowl Play

My work continued to puzzle old Annie McCrae. When I called on her in a respite of typing she would say:

'Are you not out the day?'

And would then ask me who owned the blue car: or who was the one in the red hat; or why was the milk-man so late and who was he giving the lift to? Because we lived along the road she expected we should have known. Neither Alice nor I of course had noticed. She confessed later to Alice that when I was not out I must be idling and she was afraid 'the nice Dublin man' might sack me. (On their way to Donegal Seamus Delargy and his brother Jack had given us a quick call and he had talked to Annie: she understood his Gaelic more readily than Wagner's.)

Then she revealed she was worried: her folklore had appeared to dry up and I was sure I had unintentionally offended her. While she had, as the phrase put it 'her day in the house and the use of the land' to let in conacre to the neighbours it belonged to my own landlord Dan McCrae. She had heard a rumour he intended to sell it along with the place we were living in. This if true added another worry to my own.

Perhaps she decided to forestall fact in case rumour were true and placate Dan. Would I, she asked, mind taking a fowl to him and his family in Omagh when I went to pay my rent next day. I agreed unthinkingly. I suppose I daren't have refused. Cold weather had set in with some hail and I would have to start early on the three miles to Greencastle where I caught an early bus for Omagh. I said I would call later to collect the fowl, but she said not to worry; she would be up in the morning and have it ready. And that with old Annie was that.

It was a bitter, grey morning with unmelted hail along the roadsides. I went up to Annie's to collect the fowl, aware of more hail showers trailing slow-moving curtains from the country at Gortin into Glenlark.

Annie was leaning over the half-door waiting. She handed me a black shopping-bag with the fowl in it: but alive! I had assumed she would at least have killed if not plucked and trussed it. The hen was trussed alright but only around the legs with a strip torn off an old pinafore. As the bag was too small to nest the hen fully its head and angry eyes stuck up one side and its tail up out of the other.

I took it because I didn't know how to refuse..

Alice was furious and wanted me to leave the bluddy hen and some invented explanation to herself. I was confused as well as worried and words flashed like winter lightning in the cold airs between us. I was told I was 'selling my bit of dignity as well as soul for the sake of folklore' which was maybe very true had I known it.

I left for Greencastle on the bike, slipping the handles of the bag over one handlebar. Nothing happened for a while. Walking up the long hill from Glenhull the hen waited until I reached The Nine Pipes with its fall screened by bramble. A hail shower cut down, the hen gave a squawk and before I could grab her was out of the bag, tied legs and all, and had fluttered into the hedge at the side of the bridge. I let the bicycle fall and dived after her, grabbed her at last, rammed her back into the bag when I had retrieved the bike and was cursing like a trooper – Old Annie, hens, folklore and the propitiation of its narrators, Glenhull, the hailstones and everything else. I can curse too: my grandfather John Campbell, as well as being storyteller and able country carpenter, was the best hand at it before priest, parson or polissman in our Parish at Dromintee.

The hen behaved herself until I got to Greencastle where one left the bicycle in McCullagh's open coal-shed which had a galvanised iron roof. I was alone for a while. But the bus was late and other passengers came. They stood in the open doorway looking out; I stood back with the black bag in a firm two-handed grip held behind my back. I felt a squirm and shuffle now and then and prayed to heaven the hen would keep quiet. Annie had enjoined secrecy on me: what if people gossiped that 'The Folklore Man from The Bungalow' had taken to stripping roosts (as well as being a possible Communist!) Once, the hen fidgeted and made a sound but a hail shower burst on the roof and saved me. I silently swore that whatever the outcome there would nothing in the category of this kind of 'Fowl Play' in the cause of the folk quest or neighbourly good relationship however delicately intertwined.

At last the bus came.

An hour later in Omagh I went direct to Dan McCrae's pub and dumped the bag on the bar, explained, and said I was to call back for the bag later. I hurried out. All during the hour journey I had not once relaxed a very firm grip on the mouth of the bag with the hen completely submerged and hidden inside.

'Ah sure,' says Dan as I was going out, peeping into the bag, 'begod Mick did she not pluck it?'

'You get it as I got her,' I said. As I went I saw Dan toss the bag on to a shelf. When I returned on my way to catch the return bus, the only one, Dan and his wife and son were in the bar. The hen lay on the floor – stiff and very dead.

'Begod,' says Dan hesitantly, 'she be to smother, Mick?'

'Go to hell – No?' I said back.

'Was she alive leaving?'

'Alive be damned.' I gave a swift account of the diversions. Then I said: 'Now how the hell could that happen and me nursin' her on me lap all the way in . . . ' Which was true. I didn't of course mention the death's grip.

'Ah well, sure she mightn't have bothered. No matter. Will you take a bottle of stout or a drop of whiskey, Mick?'

Paraphrasing old Francis Frank Jack in his joke at The Stations in McKenna's in Carnanransy I said:

'Try me with both.'

Dan had heard that one too. But good enough he did set up both. (Back in Glenhull I returned the bag to Annie unaware that Dan had put half-a-pint in it for her which she broached for me on the spot) but I suppressed all word of my 'fowl murder' on the way to Omagh.

32   The White Bird of The Lowlands

Francis Daniel had either exhausted all his memories of folk-stories, or his failure to recall 'The White Bird of the Lowlands' was another log damming the stream of flow. I got perturbed when, as I moved about the countryside, people smiled and smirked as they recounted – quite unknown to me – how he was visiting houses where he thought some old person might have the story – even the start of it – or a section of it.

One morning after snow showers had eased off he sent a message to me with his daughter. It was a bleak day with snow menace cowering everywhere. He wrote in a far from literate hand and wording, first with his address:

> That as the day was not so good would I please come to go to Rousky to meet a Mrs MacCullagh (a Travelling Woman of the roads I had hoped to meet) and see what she possesses. She might be of great service to me. He would be waiting.

He added that he had heard she had 'The White Bird'. As if I hadn't surmised.

Snow and sleet fell again. Alice told me I would be mad to go. But high on the other side of the glen I could see him standing against the white of the gable-end, waiting.

He was already in overcoat and with bicycle on the road when I got there. Snow fell. It began to freeze. I invited him into Eddie McCullagh's pub but he refused: only lose time. He explained that 'Tilda was a Travelling Woman alright and knew the cracks of the country'. One of his grandchildren below Rousky had heard her tell a crack about 'The White Bird' at the fireside when benighted there. She lived in a labourer's cottage below Rousky but might be in one of a dozen houses on the hillsides between us and Gortin. We would need to hurry while we had light. He ignored the snow and sleet and cold.

At Rousky chapel he paused, wondering if we should 'drop in for a mouthful of prayers', decided that time was against us and rode on. We arrived at Tilda's. She wasn't in. A man claying potato-pits hurriedly against frost said he didn't know where she might be. And of course Francis Daniel asked him if he had ever heard her tell a story about 'The White Bird of the Lowlands'. The man smiled, said he had 'heard her tell old pieces' but couldn't remember. It was all balderdash and a lot of nonsense anyhow. The news seemed to distress Francis Daniel.

I told him not to mind: we would find her some other time: better return home. There was snow in the air. No, she was somewhere near hand. He would find her. Not to worry. Old people like Tilda were liable to drop off like flies – Take the story with her.

On the hillside two houses sat far apart like frozen gulls. Would she be in one of those? As he talked a snow shower swept over the hill and blotted hill and houses out with wind-tangled curtains of white held up by invisible hands. Instead of turning back however he rode on towards Gortin. I had to follow. At a house here and there along the road he would leap off, bend, listen. 'No. That's not her voice . . . ' I was too cold to be either angry or embarrassed standing in the snow shower. On again and the same stops to listen. Suddenly I began to enjoy this caper. I suggested Gortin clearly ahead and a pub.

He turned back at once and rode like mad, ignoring another shower. At one house, shoulders white with snow, he went up a lane and actually leaned over the half-door, listening. No doubt about my embarrassment and alarm now! He strode into another house, asked for Tilda and in reply to a question announced:

'There's a folklore man from the University of Dublin would like a word with her.' I tried to correct him – the University bit however academically inaccurate – but he repeated the same phrase in another house.

We retraced, he in the lead. He pulled up so suddenly I skidded and had to drop off into the roadside. Ignoring me he dumped his bicycle, hopped up on a ditch, and then I saw a man shovelling clay to a potato-pit, so white I had not noticed him at first against the snow. There was the ruin of a thatched house beside us, the thatch-draped fallen beams forming a cave-like passageway to a door to a tinned-roof room. The door of this was closed with a crowbar and huge stones. I was told the man lived in it nevertheless.

Francis muttered to me that the man was named 'something the Clock' – he used to repair clocks and should have knowledge: a man in his 60's heavily built and belligerent-looking (maybe the biting cold) and wearing a torn hat which showed his bald skull through the crown. He didn't know where Tilda was and didn't care either.

'She might be out the back water – or in Glenlark?' ('Back water' meant the area on the far side of the river.)

'You couldn't,' says Francis, as more snow began to fall, 'be of service to this man. He's a man after folklore if you know what that means from the University of Dublin . . . '

'What the hell's folklore?' He went on claying the potatoes with his long-shafted shovel.

'Ould cracks. Stories and rehearsals. And fairy stories. Cracks about fairies.'

The man replied without ceasing his work that there never had been any such bluddy thing as fairies. Unruffled by this retort Francis went on to tell him that he was wrong: at least there used be fairies. The man denied this aggressively. Francis again assured him he was wrong: that his own mother had seen fairies. The man retorted that he didn't give a damn whose mother had seen them, they had never existed.

'Are you tryin',' says Francis, 'to tell me that my mother was a liar?'

Snow began to fall thickly but they went on arguing, the man shovelling clay and snow, Francis poised above him on the ditch. Francis was trying to convince the man of his error by reciting a fairy story and fairy event one after the other, oblivious of the snow.

I had to move else I'd stiffen. We sheltered at a gable with a busby of ivy, then rode on again. An early dusk was gathering. I said I was going home. He finally persuaded me to visit a married daughter of his living near by, where indeed we were made welcome. She confirmed she had heard Tilda tell stories but couldn't recall her telling one about our 'White Bird of the Lowlands'.

While we took tea the children, crimson-cheeked with the snow, faces alight, were in and out. One came running in blurting that Tilda had been seen going to a neighbouring house a little earlier. At once Francis was on his feet, abandoning his tea, urging the lad to run back to make sure. The lad had snow on his shoulders. I got up and said we would go ourselves. An older girl however chased out into the darkness and came back to say Tilda had headed for home.

Tilda was at home alright, with the door on the latch. Francis strode in without knock or hail, greeting her, to which she answered in a tired way. A stub of a candle, apart from the faint rising glow of a tiny fire, was the only light and I couldn't see what she looked like except in silhouette against the candle-flame: plump cheeks, strong Roman nose, the voice low, with the usual handkerchief on her head knotted under the chin. A woman who lived on the charity of the people without begging, she was walking a lonely road, the last in a long tradition of such women who told stories and gossip in return for hospitality and a bed in some corner if night found her there.

She did have stories. But she did not have 'The White Bird of the Lowlands' although she had heard the tale told in Munterloney and Park in the Sperrins in Derry.

She did tell other tales and repeatedly said 'would have more next time we called'. I was eager to go: Francis was doing all the talking: the woman must have been even more perished than I was in the cold kitchen. Her bed was in the corner. At last even he had to begin stamping his feet. We left.

He was thoroughly disgruntled on the way back, for though it was dark now the snow showed us the way, neither of us having lights. Again he refused to go into the pub at Greencastle: in fact wondered if we should ride on and call on a man further along the road. And did. The man apologised for his poor fire (A Year of Bad Firing: the new crop still on the hills and old almost exhausted). He had not stories of any kind.

It ended the quest – almost – for 'The White Bird of The Lowlands.'

33 The Broad Road Again

We were planning to return to South Armagh and my father was seeking a house for us. I reported to the Commission that while I would remain until October I intended to get my wife and family back to the Slieve Gullion country before the real onset of winter. Immediately I was requested to remain where I was. Would I care to try the following Spring in some of the areas I had noted in my BBC research – would I think of the Glens of Antrim? If so Seamus Delargy, himself a native of Cushendall, would make inquiries about a house. I left the decision to Alice. She agreed to go to Antrim in the Spring.

My Glenhull collections were well over the million words, but I collected more intensely than ever, making isolated forays into outlying districts. This brought us some odd callers, even in the middle of the night.

About 2.00 one morning a van pulled up and a voice calling wakened me. Was I Murphy the man after folklore stories? I said I was.

'I have a great story,' said the voice.

I replied that if he didn't get the hell out of there I had a better one.

Another day a man with a high-stepping gait stopped at the gate, called me out and asked if I had a cork-screw. Bottles of stout stuck out of his pocket and he had two in his hand. I brought out a cork-screw. He drew a cork and drank.

'Would you be Murphy the man after old history?'

I said I supposed I was.

He slugged the bottle empty, pulled the other, but didn't ask me had I a mouth on me.

'What,' he asked me next, 'do you think of the chiefs of the Irish clans?'

'Too many of them,' I said, watching him drain the second bottle, 'the greatest set of whore-masters in shoe-leather.'

Without taking the 'bottle off his head' he swivelled and stared at me, then back as before and drained his bottle, tossing it aside as he had done with the other.

'Tell me then,' he says, 'who do you say the O'Neill's sprung from? An' what do you say about Irish history.'

Except that it had yet to be written I said I had nothing to say. He wheeled, in his peculiar gait, walking away.

'Oh, I wouldn't discuss history with you at all, sir.' And when he was out of sight, still muttering about my ignorance, I remembered he had taken our corkscrew with him.

'The Stations' came to McCrae's at the pub and post office, again bye-passing Francis McBride. Christmas was a month away. He didn't call in as often as usual and had lost much of his gaiety: but the weather was really bad, winter setting in early, and everyone was in poor humour, many with their turf lost out on the mountains, while sudden floods in the Owenkillew carried stacks of hay which blocked the eye of the bridge at Glenhull and caused a lake to form over the holms.

But the mill kept on grinding, and I spent time getting its traditions off the miller, old Porter, lame and whimsical. He kept his few fowl roosting before his thatched house in the elder or boor-tree bushes. Jimmy O'Neill still flushed his fire to wild flame with paraffin oil.

Michael Morris called often but seemed dispirited also. He was beginning to find the social life inhibiting, the ragged ends of gossip losing initial humour when they found an extended life in petty incident and detail. He intended first to cross to London in the New Year for a while, then possibly across the Atlantic again to New York. I got the impression he hated having to make this decision: he loved his native area, knew its history, much of its ancient language, liked the people. But there was something lacking. My coming had created a stir and renewal of interest, an awareness of heritage, but everyone knew now that I was to move next year: out, as we say in South Armagh, for the broad road again: though not, as the beggarman would put it, exactly swopping priddies for prayers.

Then Morris asked me what I thought of the decision of Francis Daniel to sell his farm and emigrate to England: he presumed I had heard. The very idea seemed absurd, let alone incredible.

Some of my narrators died and I attended their wake. Francis Daniel McAleer's wife had died; Peadar Haughey in The Black Bog of Creggan among others. The urn of Glenhull with its heritage of folk secret was tipping now, slipping from the cross-belt hammock of the crossed roads.

Christmas again: still with our smoking chimney and open door. On Christmas Eve Glenhull was swaddled in frost. Blue turf smoke rose lazily in scrolls from houses along the road at Crockacanty. Weak sunlight later seemed to wander along the peaty sky-line of Formil and Aghascruba to Muninameal like some spirit lost or lamenting, disappearing behind Crockanbwee.

In fields and gaps cattle stood around the remains of sodden straw. Porter's flock of fowl had been thinned – by cold or the marauding fox or both. But the mill-wheel turned and the old mill rumbled out its own muted thunder. By evening a dull light lingered on the holms along the Owenkillew. Window lights began to appear. In South Armagh (resumed after the deprivations of war) candles would shine in every window of the houses, and in Forkill, most exquisitely sited mountain village in Ireland, Larkin's and McNamee's pubs would burst with light and laughter, with banter and song from young and old, all out on that set night. But it would be dull and gloomy and repressed in Glenhull.

I went nevertheless: sat again on the upturned cases of stout around the oil-heater. One man even knelt on one knee. They talked of Christmas and other men no longer with them. Mention of one name stilled everyone.

There was no barber in or near Glenhull, but as at home one man cut another's hair. Francis McBride used clip mine and then I would trim his, and anyone else present. There were a few in the house one night while he barbered me, the others chatting and joking Alice, amusing themselves with the children. McBride had not regained his impish sense of humour and we thought it was all due to the weather.

He whispered in my ear:

'This might be the last time I might cut your hair. You may be gone. I think I might have to go into the hospital again for a while . . . '

He had had a recurrence of an old trouble but I hadn't heard.

One evening walking up the hill at The Nine Pipes I stood in to let a car pass, saw that one of the passengers was Francis, waved, and he barely looked up as he diffidently waved a reply. Less than a month later his son came to our house one pouring Sunday morning, stood, refused tea (and I noticed he had nicked himself shaving) and then told me he had bad news.

His father was dead.

I remember feeling stunned. I remembered the night he had cut my hair the odd prophetic words he had said which I ascribed to his despondency.

Did he know? The skies opened as if aware of the passing of one gay, light-hearted soul and were mourning along with the whole parish. I remember hurrying up to Annie McCrae, finding her on her knees on the hearthstone, bent across a chair, her Rosary in her hands. She was a woman who had seen much death and calamity in her family, was now alone for sixteen years, yet her eyes were full of weeping. She got up, couldn't speak, but shook my hand in both her own. I remembered I had even forgotten to shake the hand of Francis Henry in sympathy.

In the rain in the afternoon figures in shawls and top coats went to his wake. I saw a man take the near-cut across the holm and use the stilts which Francis could handle so athletically. There was something so imponderable about the passing of this man that it impeded thought . . . His great sense of humour? Zest for life and people and custom? His gaiety and banter? Something unanalytical still . . . ?

In a constant downpour we buried Francis McBride in his family grave beneath Solo's Tree in the graveyard at Greencastle. The whole countryside was shrouded in sheets of rain. Burns rushed in a shroud-brown froth. Not a beast was to be seen in any field. I stood there with Michael Morris. Gusts in the trees made our lament and shook a spatter of raindrops on to the coffin to shed tears for the people.

On the morning after his funeral the sky became bright and breezy. Snow had fallen again in the night following the rain. The Owenkillew was in spate sometimes in blue, then black, and at the bend at McBride's land wore serpentine lacery of froth like a frill on a dress. I looked towards the end of his loanan as a tractor went by.

His son, Francis Henry, was carrying the empty creamery can on his back up to the house. It used to be the chore of his father.

34 The First Farewell

Seamus Delargy had found a place for me at Layde on the braeside overlooking Red Bay and Cushendall in Antrim. I would go in early spring. More of my storytellers died. Michael Morris left for London. Francis Daniel had sold his farm and with his family was already in Middlesboro in England. I thought I had better move around those of my narrators who remained in a visit of farewell and grateful thanks: they had endured months of conversational querying from me: the volumes were filled with the voices of the living and the dead – and the dead I had never known in the flesh.

It was still difficult to imagine McBride gone. His death had taken from the place a definite spirit and mood he personified; Morris and others had felt the same sense of abrupt vacancy, as if his spirit had not been properly appreciated while he lived. It is always so with rich character of any kind.

Annie McCrae was distressed. She epitomised what a few others had said when she told me frankly that she would 'pray we wouldn't get a house in Antrim and we would maybe stay on, but that if we did that it might be a good one and have the height of good luck and health in it.'

No longer could she narrate a single item: everything, she claimed, had again left her head. She always lamented for McBride and his quick, light step and told us how much he thought of us and what I was doing. She liked our children and they liked her. One day she said to me:

'I couldn't stick it here after yous leave. I'll go into the Home in Derry. I won't live long now anyhow. I'm prepared. I have all the Masses paid for.' And she added: 'An' poor wee Peter'll be in the far County Antrim an' wantin' to go up the lane to "Anne A'Crae." Do you think will he ever mind me . . . ? The other boys might, but I wonder will Peter when I'm not in the land o' the livin' anymore?'

I visited as many of the people as weather allowed: a chore I really did not like. There was something strange and holding about this kind of leave-taking: I once thought I should try to slip away unnoticed. But I was still more than a fellow from South Armagh and had more than a social duty to perform. Persistently that imponderable, frustrating and elusive thing dogged every thought.

I left the visit to Padraig McCullagh to the last. This was one of the most outstanding characters of his kind I was ever likely to meet. I think I really dreaded taking farewell of him.

He came instead one night to see me. Casually he mentioned that he had heard I was leaving, and right off went on to tell some lore he had forgotten to mention: because hardly on a single aspect of folk tradition could one ask a question without Padraig Phelimy being able to give a reply.

He told of poteen-makers: and as he was an expert himself told one of his own tales. He deplored the substitutes and adulterations used in latter-day washes; if he couldn't get barley around Omagh or in Derry he quietly had it railed from Dundalk. Dubious substances were not for him, although each had its own vernacular term in folklore.

He was caught once and told the tale with occasional chuckles – proudly. Police broke up his barrels in Fallagh Glen a few times, but as he was a cooper as well as everything else Padraig, in hiding while they were around, had the barrels together before they were on the road. But caught with his poteen he was tried in Cookstown. Without rancour but with the pride of integrity he told how the prosecuting District Inspector of police stated that analysis of the poteen captured was, as Padraig put it himself 'the purest and strongest ever seized in Tyrone.' He was fined ten pounds. Once the episcopal decree was issued he ceased the traffic at once.

He left about 1.00 in the morning. I had shown him the stack of copies of the volumes I had roughly bound for transport, as a gesture of thanks and appreciation. He dismissed them casually and said there was 'twice as much more if we had time to get it.' But he said he was very glad to know so much had been written at last, and blamed his own memory for having forgotten so much.

Suddenly he remarked that he must be keeping us out of bed. He shook hands with Alice, wished her luck and happiness, thanked her, and when she made some jocose comment laughed in his quick, shy, husky way. He looked round to shake hands with the children, forgetting they had been put to bed. I saw him to the road.

He was still wearing the old raincoat. We talked. I didn't know what to say. Again he said he must be keeping me out of bed, an idea I honestly dismissed. I wonder if he had some feelings to suppress as I certainly had at that moment? For he grabbed my hand in his powerful grip, shook it, He looked at me. Said nothing for a while. Then huskily wished me the 'height of good luck.' That I 'deserved it.' Showered praises on me and how I had gone about my job. I had done a 'great days' work.' Some day we might meet again. And as impulsive as in his speech leaped on his bicycle and was gone.

I stood looking into the darkness after him. I was reluctant to go inside. In my mind I could see the coat tails flying from him on the unlighted bicycle – past Glenhull bridge and old Kirke's – past the bridge at Coneyglen, up the hill, rattling down the long run to the bridge at Altacamcosy and along the narrow winding road of dips and hollows into Curraghinalt.

He must have been near home when Alice stood silhouetted in the light in our doorway. I went inside and sat and smoked but didn't talk.

She didn't press me. I noticed she had already taken down some small items from the walls – a holy-water font, a calendar with a picture she liked, a pouch for letter and note-paper.

That sense of vacancy and vacuum of flitting once more.

35   The Folk Mind Closes

I had gone to Layde. The house needed some repair which could not be done immediately. We would not be far off the sea; and we loved the sea.

Francis Daniel's long folk-story which had been recorded by the BBC in Belfast came on the air in a series on 'The Irish Storyteller' broadcast from London. People who had never heard the man, who jibed at the idea of his having such ability, expressed amazement at his powers, but I could see some of them far from pleased at the way he refused to euphemise earthy comment and bowdlerise the story as told in the original.

Annie McCrae had almost completely withdrawn into herself: almost as withdrawn as she had been on that first day when she took me for a bold-necked Travelling Man come to frighten and impose upon her. And curiously Glenhull seemed to be strange to me, resentful again, hostile even. Not as an intruder now, but as a deserter.

April came, and with it a symbol of the end of the quest in Glenhull if I were seeking one. On a day of dry, loping winds the old thatched roof of Francis Daniel's house was on fire. It burned for two nights. At night the red glow would burst into flames which capered across the thatch in gay but malicious mimicry of figures from some of his own tales – fitful, fiery, red. In the day-time the smoke curled reluctantly over the graph of his turf banks which wrinkled the high brow of Muninameal. It seemed to shroud old, weary and confused souls released into a world they no longer understood. The smoke wafted this way and that, gathered into a huddle like sheep before a summer storm, then strolled in a long continuous column up the fields above the house, over the heather, over the turf-bank on the brow, up and over the summit, thinning as it went.

I remembered the nights in his house, his family and his wife, her wake, his auction and his departure for England to another kind of smoke and grime in Middlesboro. The uprootment of such a man from his environment again depressed me like an omen for a whole people and not Glenhull alone, but still a fact too preposterous to be tragic. And yet it was like a kind of fantastic Death: the body deserting the soul to leave it in a trance like an event from one of his own folk-stories. One felt that some day the soul, as in the story, must somehow reunite with the body, as the spirit in the smoke in its nebulous way was making communion with the fields and hillside and heights of which all were one.

Worse than all, as I watched, it epitomised the tragedy of the depopulation of a country. In mimicry of another of his tales it seemed that the kernel of eternal truth in all folklore showed a malignant Fate decreeing that Ireland and her people, her culture and their spiritual heritage must again and again undergo this fantasy of protracted agony before a delusion of Death, to be resuscitated at the last moment and rise, only to die the Death of delusion once more, exhausted in body and soul.

I still have the letter I received from him hardly before the ashes of the roof were cool: He had remembered his 'White Bird of The Lowlands.' He was writing it down for me. He added: 'My heart's in the old stories more than ever.' And he missed hearing the broadcast of his own story from London. A last line touched the heart and unreality: 'Does anyone keep a fire in the hearth in the old home?' He hadn't heard of the burning.

Annie McCrea wanted to believe that because my move to Antrim had been delayed, we were not going to move at all until a 'Notice To Let' appeared in the local paper out of Omagh.

The night before we left there was a good moon in a calm sky. Light touched the elbows of the bends of the Owenkillew below our house and brought a feeling of an intense peace following a compressed period of tumult: it was as if ages had been surging through the glen since I had come. Having fulfilled its duty to the past by holding on to Life while I raced like the man in the folktale who outwitted Death by a trick I seemed to understand just how exhausted I had become: I could no longer engage in any casual conversation anywhere without the memory recording some folk fact.

Maybe I deluded myself that I could breathe in a peace which had now found a new breath of its own while it waited the arrival of the signs and wonders – and fears – of a new age.

36 End of a Quest

One day in May we left Glenhull for Layde in Antrim. Everything had gone ahead – except for some odd reason – the clock; Alice carried it in a shopping bag. Neighbours and friends the night before had called with gifts of eggs, of fowl, of butter. We were to get picked up by a car at Carnan bridge and walked up the road.

Annie McCrae was leaning over her half-door until she spotted us and withdrew at once. In a field below the road we saw Sarah McBride, the wife of Francis. She hadn't expected to see us and turned her back at once. She had said:

'I don't want to see you leave. You're never to say good-bye on the day they leave to anyone you care for and think a lot of. You're to watch them go from a distance and not let yourself be seen.'

Before we came to Carnan bridge I stopped and looked back . . . and Alice had to call and remind me that the car might be due.

A lifetime seemed to have swept by since that December day we had arrived. I suddenly felt at once elated, sad, and very tired.

37 The Return

I did not return to Glenhull until twelve years later with my friend Sam Hanna Bell of the BBC.

Driving in from Cookstown it seemed landmarks were extraordinarily reluctant to show up: but by then I had hundreds of Ulster road-miles behind me, including the single stretch on Rathlin Island. Glenhull looked lonelier than ever despite changes and a new red-brick bungalow in conventional style built near the road. Our 'Bungalow' had not changed, apart from a new front door with a glass panel, but was closed again. McCrae's bar had been modernised. I was recognised here and there, hailed, and shaken warmly by the hand.

Annie McCrae's spotless kitchen now stabbed blackened gables at the sky. One morning neighbours had discovered her standing in the street with her clothes on fire and the house ablaze. She went to the Home in Derry and had died there.

Old Francis Frank Jack and his kindly wife were dead: Sarah McBride also, John Donnelly at 'The head of the Town': he had ploughed that headrig he had figuratively mentioned. It was impossible not to recall the man Francis McBride: expect to see his spritely figure appear somewhere with a joke on his lips.

The old road in Glenlark had been surfaced with tarmacadam, but all the people I had known there were dead. Across the river from Gorticashel we went to Curraghinalt. In a field beside Padraig McCullagh's lay a heap of sand and mortar intended for use in renovation of the house; but it was weed-covered, the house itself a collapsed shambles; and Padraig Phelimy dead and buried in Rousky along with his sister. I could not help wonder what he might have said had he lived to see his rush-woven harness on display by The National Museum in Dublin. In the ruins of his house were found part of another set half-completed and intended for The Ulster Folk Museum at Cultra.

Old Porter the Miller was gone, the mill itself adapted to the making of concrete blocks, its massive wheel silent and still. Michael Morris had gone from London to the United States. But Mal McAleer, working in one of his roadside fields near that little well saw us, ran, and lithely came over the barbed-wire. It was hard to break off the conversation, so much to say, so little said.

Outside the pub at Glenhull I stood alone. I remembered Francis Daniel's roof on fire, the living fantasy of the separated personality of his emigration, the smoke commingling with the spirit of field and hillside. Jimmy O'Neill dead too. I stood and stared as if hoping to recognise some lost composite image in which part of myself was woven. I may have gone through roads in Old Ulster from Rathlin to The Boyne, collecting volumes of lore. But it had really begun here in Glenhull: I had the notion that this return would reveal some of the elusive mystery of it all and reassure me of the worth of what I was doing. Outside McCrae's pub I stood and stared and tried to dream.

Alice had refused to come back: had advised me not to go. Now I began to see why. I had sent down roots into the life and earth of this glen as I had done in South Armagh. When I left twelve years ago I had not pulled them up, merely snapped them off. They still remained, stunted maybe, unfamiliar now, but still alive.

Alice had told me one can never go back. But I knew part of me had never left.

I remembered the folktale of The Man Who Outwitted Death. The Angel had waited here or I had outpaced it long enough to hear the last voices confess the folk heritage before it outran us all and claimed its own.

But not to silence. Like the fugitive part of me in Glenhull they would now live for ever.

I was not surprised to hear that the great storyteller Francis Daniel had returned to Tyrone, although it was to an Old Men's Home.

THE END